Mary, Queen of Scots

'In my end is my beginning'

Mary, Queen of Scots

'In my end is my beginning'

Rosalind K. Marshall

MARY, QUEEN
OF SCOTS

First published in 2013 by
NMS Enterprises Limited – Publishing
a division of NMS Enterprises Limited
National Museums Scotland
Chambers Street
Edinburgh EH1 1JF

www.nms.ac.uk

British Library Cataloguing in Publication Data
A catalogue record for this book
is available from the British Library.

ISBN (cased):   978 1 905267 82 8
ISBN (paper):   978 1 905267 78 1

Book layout and design by Mark Blackadder.
Printed and bound in the United Kingdom
by Bell & Bain Limited, Glasgow.

For a full listing of NMS Enterprises Limited
Publishing titles and related merchandise:
www.nms.ac.uk/books

EXHIBITION SPONSORED BY

INVESTMENT MANAGERS

National Museums Scotland would like to thank
Baillie Gifford Investment Managers
for their generous sponsorship of this Exhibition.

The Museum is extremely grateful for their support.

CONTENTS

MARY, QUEEN
OF SCOTS

Mary, Queen of Scots
  by Rosalind K. Marshall

COVER IMAGES

Front: *The Blairs Memorial
Portrait of Mary, Queen of
Scots* (1542–87).
CATALOGUE NO. 1

Back: A gold locket with
a French or Italian cameo
of Mary, Queen of Scots
(late 16th century).
CATALOGUE NO. 91

EXHIBITION CREDITS

Mary, Queen of Scots

National Museum of Scotland
Chambers Street
Edinburgh EH1 1JF

28 June to 17 November 2013

www.nms.ac.uk

EXHIBITION CREDITS

Thanks are due to previous and current staff of National Museums Scotland who have contributed to the Exhibition and who have assisted with this publication.

Thanks are also due to Dr Rosalind K. Marshall for her contribution to this publication and her kind assistance and advice throughout this project.

EXHIBITION LOANS

National Museums Scotland would like to thank the following organisations and individuals for their assistance as lenders to this Exhibition:

Addyman Archaeology
Bibliothèque nationale de France, Paris
Blair Castle, Perthshire
Blairs Museum
The British Library
The British Museum
The British Province of the Society of Jesus
The Bute Collection at Mount Stuart
Victoria Cairns
His Grace the Archbishop of Canterbury and the Trustees of Lambeth Palace Library
The Church of England: St Stephen's Church, St Albans
Jasper Conran OBE
Dundee City Council
Lord Egremont
The Faculty of Advocates
Sir Angus Grossart
His Grace, The Duke of Hamilton, Lennoxlove, Haddington
The Lady Herries of Terregles
Historic Scotland
The Earl of Mar and Kellie
Mr and Mrs Geoffrey Munn
Musée du Louvre, Paris
The National Archives, UK

The National Library of Scotland
National Portrait Gallery, London
National Records of Scotland
His Grace The Duke of Norfolk
Perth Museum & Art Gallery, Perth & Kinross Council
Private Collections
Royal Collection Trust on behalf of Her Majesty Queen Elizabeth II
Royal College of Music, London
Scottish National Portrait Gallery, Edinburgh
The Thomson Collection
Victoria and Albert Museum, London
The descendants of Sir John Young of Leny

FOREWORD

Dr Gordon Rintoul
DIRECTOR, NATIONAL MUSEUMS SCOTLAND

THIS Mary, Queen of Scots exhibition is the most comprehensive one to be held for a great many decades. It is also the first to bring together a diverse range of artefacts including jewellery, textiles, furniture, paintings, drawings, maps and documents to illustrate the life and times of one of the most famous and controversial characters in Scottish history.

The extensive selection of around two hundred objects has been drawn from the collections of National Museums Scotland, augmented with many loans from major public collections in Scotland, England and France, and a number of key private lenders, whose families often had direct links to Mary and her era.

Mary, Queen of Scots continues to spark debate. We hope that we will help to throw new light on this remarkable Scottish Queen and bring her story and legacy to life through this unique exhibition.

BELOW

A detail from the
Morton Valances.
French and/or Scottish,
c.1580–90
CATALOGUE NO. 101

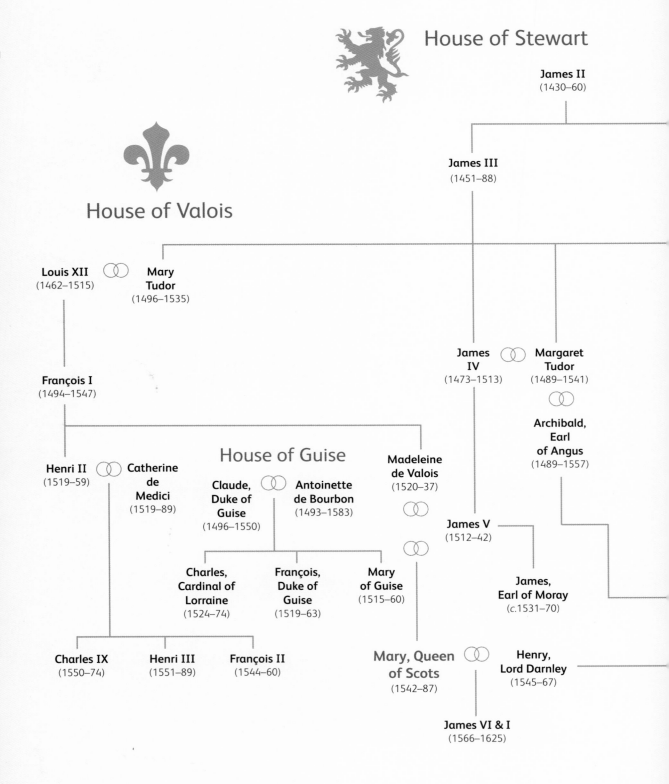

House of Stewart

James II
(1430–60)

James III
(1451–88)

House of Valois

Louis XII ⬭⬭ **Mary Tudor**
(1462–1515)   (1496–1535)

James IV ⬭⬭ **Margaret Tudor**
(1473–1513)   (1489–1541)

⬭⬭

Archibald, Earl of Angus
(1489–1557)

François I
(1494–1547)

House of Guise

Madeleine de Valois
(1520–37)

Henri II ⬭⬭ **Catherine de Medici**
(1519–59)   (1519–89)

Claude, Duke of Guise ⬭⬭ **Antoinette de Bourbon**
(1496–1550)   (1493–1583)

⬭⬭

James V
(1512–42)

Charles, Cardinal of Lorraine
(1524–74)

François, Duke of Guise
(1519–63)

Mary of Guise
(1515–60)

⬭⬭

James, Earl of Moray
(c.1531–70)

Charles IX
(1550–74)

Henri III
(1551–89)

François II
(1544–60)

Mary, Queen of Scots ⬭⬭ **Henry, Lord Darnley**
(1542–87)   (1545–67)

James VI & I
(1566–1625)

House of Tudor

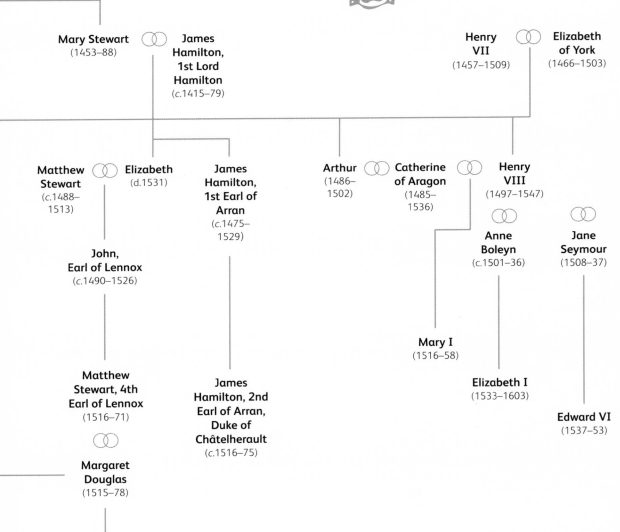

Mary Stewart
(1453–88)

⬭⬭

James Hamilton, 1st Lord Hamilton
(*c.*1415–79)

Henry VII
(1457–1509)

⬭⬭

Elizabeth of York
(1466–1503)

Matthew Stewart
(*c.*1488–1513)

⬭⬭

Elizabeth
(d.1531)

James Hamilton, 1st Earl of Arran
(*c.*1475–1529)

Arthur
(1486–1502)

⬭⬭

Catherine of Aragon
(1485–1536)

⬭⬭

Henry VIII
(1497–1547)

⬭⬭

Anne Boleyn
(*c.*1501–36)

⬭⬭

Jane Seymour
(1508–37)

John, Earl of Lennox
(*c.*1490–1526)

Mary I
(1516–58)

Matthew Stewart, 4th Earl of Lennox
(1516–71)

⬭⬭

Margaret Douglas
(1515–78)

James Hamilton, 2nd Earl of Arran, Duke of Châtelherault
(*c.*1516–75)

Elizabeth I
(1533–1603)

Edward VI
(1537–53)

LIST OF ILLUSTRATIONS

X

- John Knox, *First Blast of the Trumpet against the Monstrous Regiment of Women*, 1558, his tract aimed against Europe's Catholic women rulers, especially Mary Tudor and Mary of Guise. (© National Library of Scotland)

- *George Buchanan (1506–82), historian, poet and Reformer*, by an unknown artist, late 16th century. (© Scottish National Portrait Gallery)

27: *Henry Stewart, Lord Darnley (1545–67)*, attributed to Levina Teerlinc (*c*.1510–76), 1560. (The Thomson Collection)

28: Darnley or Lennox Jewel, *c*.1571-78 (Royal Collection Trust/© Her Majesty Queen Elizabeth II 2013)

29: King Henry and Queen Mary silver ryal, Edinburgh, 1565. (National Museums Scotland)

30: *James Douglas, 4th Earl of Morton (1516–81)*, attributed to Arnold Bronckorst, *c*.1580. (© Scottish National Portrait Gallery.) Not in exhibition.

31: *Henry Stewart, Lord Darnley (1545–67)*, by an unknown artist, *c*.1564. (© Scottish National Portrait Gallery)

36: Order from Craigmillar Castle to the Treasurer to supply taffeta for the baptism of Prince James, 3 December 1566. (© National Records of Scotland, E 23/3/18)

40–41: *Bird's eye view of Kirk o' Field*, 1567, sent to William Cecil in London, showing the sequence of events when Darnley was murdered. (© The National Archives, MPF 1/366/1)

42: A placard representing Mary, Queen of Scots and the Earl of Bothwell as a mermaid and a hare, 1567. (The National Archives, SP 52/13/60)

43: Fragments of 16th-century painted and glazed French earthenware, found during 2010 archaeological dig at Kirk o' Field. (By kind permission of George Haggarty)

46: *James Hepburn, 4th Earl of Bothwell (c.1535–78)*, by an unknown artist, 1566. (© Scottish National Portrait Gallery)

48: Sketch of a banner design used by the Lords of the Congregation at Carberry Hill, during their confrontation with Mary, Queen of Scots, 15 June 1567. (The National Archives, MPF 1/366/3)

49: Encounter at Carberry Hill, with Mary, Queen of Scots riding down to surrender to Sir William Kirkcaldy of Grange, a watercolour, 15 June 1567. (The National Archives, MPF 1/366/2)

- *James VI and I as a child (1566–1625)*, by Arnold Bronckorst (*c*.1574) (© Scottish National Portrait Gallery.) Not in exhibition.

50: *The Memorial of Lord Darnley*, painted by Livinus de Vogelaare, 1567. (Royal Collection Trust/© Her Majesty Queen Elizabeth II 2013)

52: The Herries Book of Hours, believed to have been left by Mary, Queen of Scots at Terregles on her last night in Scotland. (By kind permission of The Lady Herries of Terregles)

53: Inventory of books, ornaments and masquing clothes left behind by Mary, Queen of Scots when she fled to England, 1569. (© National Records of Scotland E 35/10)

- *William Cecil, 1st Baron Burghley (1520–98)*, by an unknown artist, *c*.1585. (© National Portrait Gallery, London)

54: The Lennoxlove Casket. (© Lennoxlove House Ltd. Licensor www.scran.ac.uk)

56: Plan of Tutbury Castle, by John Somers, 31 December 1584. (© The British Library Board, MS 33594 f174)

- The Marian Hanging, 1570–85. Canvas work panels embroidered by Mary, Queen of Scots and others during Mary's captivity. (© National Trust Images/ John Hammond. On loan from the Victoria and Albert Museum, London.)

57: *Sir Francis Walsingham (c.1532–90)*, possibly after John de Critz the Elder, *c*.1587, Queen Elizabeth's spy-master, in charge of intercepting the secret correspondence of Mary, Queen of Scots. (© National Portrait Gallery, London)

58: *The Trial of Mary, Queen of Scots*, ink sketch, 15 October 1586. (© The British Library Board, MS 48027 f669)

- Copy of the Death Warrant of Mary, Queen of Scots, 1 February 1587. The original warrant has disappeared, but this copy was sent to Henry Grey, 6th Earl of Kent, one of the two commissioners who organised the execution. (© Lambeth Palace Library/ MS 4769)

59: *The Execution of Mary, Queen of Scots*, early 17th century (*c*.1613), watercolour by an unknown artist. (© Scottish National Portrait Gallery)

60: *The Execution of Mary, Queen of Scots*, 8 February 1587, ink and pencil sketch, by an unknown artist. (© The British Library Board, MS 48027 f650)

61: *James VI and I (1566–1625)*, by John de Critz, 1604. Painted the year after James VI inherited the throne of England, he is shown wearing in his hat the jewel commemorating the union of the crowns, 'The Mirror of Great Britain'. (© Scottish National Portrait Gallery)

CHAPTER I
To France and Back

2

OPPOSITE PAGE

*The Blairs Memorial
Portrait of
Mary, Queen of Scots*
(1542–87).

*Artist unknown,
early 17th century*

CATALOGUE NO. 1

For details of items illustrated
in these chapters, see the
Exhibition Catalogue
(page 62)

WHEN you hear the words 'Mary, Queen of Scots', do you visualise a tall figure in black, with a white headdress, a ruff around her neck and a gold cross? That is how she is often portrayed, and indeed one of the most famous paintings shows her dressed in precisely this way. Of course, as its name suggests, the *Blairs Memorial Portrait* had a very particular purpose. It depicts her standing on the scaffold in Fotheringhay Castle, Northamptonshire, a serene figure who has vanquished death by dying a martyr for her faith. In her right hand she holds up a large crucifix, in her other hand is a prayer book, and hanging around her neck are two long strings of gold rosary beads, with a second, small crucifix suspended from a black ribbon on her bodice.

In the background of the picture, to the left, is a vignette showing the moment she placed her neck on the block and the executioner raised his axe. Another small scene at the opposite side shows two of her chamber-women in attitudes of grief. One of them, Jane Kennedy, holds a white cloth which probably represents the one she had bound round the Queen's eyes as she knelt at the block. The other, Elizabeth Curle, clasps her hands in prayer. It was she who commissioned this painting some years later while she was living in exile in Antwerp, and its meaning is made doubly clear. Mary's large coat of arms in the top left-hand corner proclaims her royal status, while three prominent inscriptions in Latin once again emphasise the fact that she was a queen in her own right. Her trial had no legal validity because of that, the inscriptions assert, and 'she always was, and is, a daughter of the Roman Church'.

The execution of the Queen of Scots took place on 8 February 1587 and people have been arguing about her ever since, for her story is endlessly intriguing. Her life had all the elements of a dramatic novel: bereavement, adultery, murder and rape, played out against a back-

MARIA SCOTIÆ REGINA, GALLIÆ DOTARIA REGNORV
ANGLIÆ ET HYBERNIÆ VERÆ PRINCEPS LEGITIMA,
IACOBI MAGNÆ BRITANIÆ REGIS MATER, A SVIS
OPPRESSA AN° DÑI 1568 AVXILII SPE ET OPINIONE A
COGNATA ELIZABETHA IN ANGLIA REGNANTE PMISSI
EÒ DESCENDIT, IBIQVE CONTRA IVS GENTIVM ET
PROMISSI FIDEM CAPTIVA RETENTA, POSTCAPTI
VITATIS AN° 19, RELIGIONIS ERGO, EIVSDEM ELIZ
PERFIDIA ET SENATVS ANGLICI CRVDELITATE,
HORRENDA CAPITIS LATA SENTENTIA NECI
TRADITVR, AC 12.CAL.MARTII 1587 IN
AVDITO EXEMPLO A SERVILI ET ABIEC
TO CARNIFICE TETRV IN MOREM CA
PITE TRVNCATA EST. ANNO ÆTATIS
REGNIQVE 45

IOANNA ELIZABETHA
KENNETHIE CVRLE.

REGINAM SERENISS¹ REGVM FILIAM,
VXOREM ET MATREM, ASTANTIBVS
COMMISSARIIS ET MINISTRIS R
ELIZABETHÆ CARIFEX SECVRI
PERCVTIT ATQ; VNO ET ALTERO
ICTV TRVCVLENTER SAVCIATÆ
TERTIO EI CAPVT ABSCINDIT,

AVLA FODRINGHAMII,

PRIMA QVOAD VIXIT COL .SCOT. PARENS. ET FVND.

SIC FVNESTVM ASCENDIT TABVLATVM REGINA QVONDAM
GALLIARV ET SCOTIÆ FLORENTIS:ᴹᴬ INVICTO SED PIO
ANIMO TYRANNIDEM EXPROBRAT ET PERFIDIAM.
FIDEM CATHOLICAM PROFITETVR, ROMANÆ₍ ECCLESIÆ
SE SEMPER FVISSE ET ESSE FILIAM PALAM PLANE₍ TESTATVR

ground of religious conflict, and culminating in long and dreary years of imprisonment. Such were her troubled times that few of her personal possessions have survived, and so the portraits, the jewellery, the prayer books and the documents which have come down to us are all the more valuable in allowing us to glimpse the reality of a larger-than-life figure, the alluring, emotional and intelligent young woman whose actions have had people speculating about her intentions for more than four hundred years.

Mary was the sole surviving child of James V, King of Scots, and his second French wife, Mary of Guise. James was said to have had at least eleven illegitimate children before his first marriage to a very prestigious bride, Madeleine de Valois, the daughter of King François I of France. Sadly, she was suffering from tuberculosis when she came to Scotland as his bride, and she died in his arms on 7 July 1537, within weeks of her arrival. Almost immediately, James was writing to his father-in-law in the hope of securing a replacement wife. He wanted to marry Madeleine's younger sister, Marguerite. However, François I had no desire to lose a second daughter to Scotland and instead he offered the eldest daughter of his close friend Claude, Duke of Guise, the head of a highly influential family. Mary of Guise was almost like another daughter to him and, what was more, she had recently been widowed. She and James could console one another. Better still, she was tall and well-built and she had already given proof that she could bear sons. Sadly, the younger died when he was only a few months old, but the other was a healthy child.

Mary of Guise was horrified when she heard about the proposed marriage, for it would mean leaving her small son behind in France. He had inherited his father's titles of Duke of Longueville and Grand Chamberlain of France, and his future lay at the French court. However, it was not possible to disobey a royal command and Mary of Guise sailed reluctantly to Scotland to become the Queen Consort of James V. A portrait of them painted shortly after their marriage shows them standing together, he in a black velvet court bonnet and gown, with a gold-trimmed doublet, she in a cloth of gold dress, her hair partly concealed by a fashionable gold and jewel-encrusted snood. They would have two sons, both of whom died in infancy, within hours of each other, and from then onwards James's situation went from bad to worse.

ABOVE

A carved ceiling medallion head of James V, King of Scots (1512–42) from Stirling Castle.

Dated c.1540

CATALOGUE NO. 14

LEFT

Mary of Guise
(1515–60).

By Corneille de Lyon,
c.*1537*

SCOTTISH NATIONAL
PORTRAIT GALLERY

BELOW

Wedding portrait
of James V and
Mary of Guise.

Artist unknown, c.*1538*

CATALOGUE NO. 3

Henry VIII of England, who was his uncle, was enraged at James's refusal to end Scotland's traditional alliance with France, which he saw as a perpetual threat to his own country. He was equally annoyed when James ignored all his demands that he, too, should follow England's example and sever the Scottish Church's ties with Rome. In the autumn of 1542, losing patience, Henry sent his army north with the intention of invading Scotland. His forces defeated the Scots at the Battle of Solway Moss, and though James was not present he seems to have suffered a complete nervous collapse. He retired to his palace of Falkland in Fife and the final blow came when word arrived that his pregnant Queen had given birth at Linlithgow Palace to a daughter instead of the much desired son. Tradition has it that when he heard the news, he turned his face to the wall and died. At six days old, the infant Princess Mary became Queen of Scots.

Obviously a regent would be required to rule Scotland throughout her childhood, and the man chosen was James Hamilton, Earl of Arran, descendant of a much earlier Stewart princess and heir presumptive to the Scottish throne. The only surviving portrait of him was painted in later life, but it hints at his shifty, unreliable character. With the English army poised to invade, he negotiated the Treaties of Greenwich with

Henry VIII, arranging that the little queen would marry Henry's young son and heir, Prince Edward. Mary of Guise and many Scots, however, opposed this agreement and the following year the Scottish Parliament cancelled the treaties. Furious, Henry launched a series of invasions which came to be known as 'The Rough Wooing', his soldiers burning and looting as they attempted to force the Scots to adhere to the terms of the treaties. Particularly painful was the occasion when they burned Holyrood Abbey, where the husband of Mary of Guise and their two infant sons were buried, and carried off the fine eagle lectern, a gift from Pope Alexander VI.

During these dangerous times, Queen Mary remained in her mother's care. Usually the heir to the Scottish throne was brought up in a different place from his parents, for reasons of security, but Mary of Guise was terrified that her daughter would be kidnapped and handed over to the English, and so she kept the little girl by her side. As a result the two developed a close and affectionate relationship.

Henry VIII died in 1547, but the situation did not improve. The Duke of Somerset, as Regent for young Edward VI, continued the series of invasions, while the Scots sought the help of their old allies, the French. On 7 July 1548 a new marriage treaty was signed near Haddington. Mary, Queen of Scots would marry the Dauphin François, the son and heir of the French king, Henri II, and in preparation for her new role, she would be brought up at the French court. This was a usual enough arrangement for royal brides, but not for a queen in her own right. However, Henri was an old friend of Mary of Guise and she knew that her child would be safer in France. As for the Regent Arran, he gave his agreement when Henri II bribed him with the French dukedom of Châtelherault.

King Henri was not, of course, planning his son's marriage out of friendly concern for Mary of Guise. In the forefront of his mind was the fact that, as the great-niece of Henry VIII and the great-grand-daughter of Henry VII, Mary, Queen of Scots had a good claim to the English throne. She and the Dauphin François might one day rule

ABOVE

A gold sovereign of Henry VIII of England (1497–1547).

Minted in London, 1509–44

CATALOGUE NO. 27

LEFT

The eagle lectern from the Abbey Church of Holyrood.

Early 16th century

CATALOGUE NO. 25

7

over not only France and Scotland, but England as well. Henri lost no time in sending one of his royal galleys to collect his future daughter-in-law, and on 29 July 1548 there was a painful parting when five-year-old Mary said goodbye to her mother in Dumbarton. 'The old queen doth lament the young queen's departure,' an English spy reported.

A series of storms blew up, and so the royal galley and its escorting vessels did not set sail until 7 August. With Mary, Queen of Scots went a large company of noblemen, aristocratic children and the Scots who

RIGHT

A Treasurer's Account recording payment for the recruitment of sailors for galleys taking Mary, Queen of Scots to France.

July 1548

CATALOGUE NO. 4

BELOW

King Henri II of France (1519–59).

By François Clouet

PALAZZO PITTI, FLORENCE, ITALY/
THE BRIDGEMAN ART LIBRARY

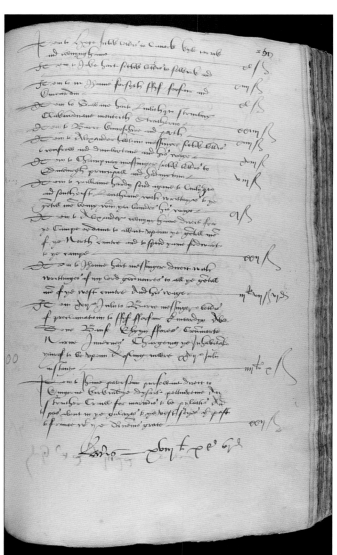

would form members of her household. There was her aunt, Lady Fleming, who would be in charge of the servants; her old nurse, Jean Sinclair, who would stay with her too; and the famous Four Maries, girls of about her own age who would be her maids-of-honour: Mary Fleming, Mary Seton, Mary Livingston and Mary Beaton.

The little queen received an enthusiastic welcome when she arrived at St Germain-en-Laye, the royal residence where Henri II and his children were waiting to meet her. The king was impressed. His future daughter-in-law was tall, sturdy and very intelligent. The only problem was that she did not speak French. Her mother had made sure that her first language was Scots, for how could you have a Queen of Scots who spoke only a foreign language? Meanwhile, the Dauphin, two years younger than Mary, became her faithful admirer. Often described as sickly and undersized, he appears in a fine enamel miniature by Léonard Limosin as a plump and healthy child. No doubt artistic licence played its part.

For the next nine and a half years, Mary was brought up with the French royal children, moving with them from one elegant, luxurious royal residence to the next, receiving the Renaissance education judged to be appropriate for a queen. She had lessons in Latin and Greek, Italian and Spanish, she had inherited the Guise love of music and, in her new environment, soon became fluent in French. Her separation from her mother was truly painful, but Mary of Guise wrote to her, received frequent reports of her progress, oversaw the expenditure of her household and the appointment of its attendants, and indeed visited France for almost a year in 1550–51. This was partly because she wanted Henri II to support her bid to wrest the regency of Scotland from the Duke of Châtelherault, but also because she was anxious to spend time with her daughter and the son of her first marriage, the teenage Duke of Longueville. Sadly, the Duke died at the end of her stay, but when she left France it was with promises of another visit before long.

Meanwhile, regular messengers continued to go to and fro between the Scottish and the French courts, and as the months passed Mary of Guise began describing the leading Scottish personalities in her letters to her daughter and gradually introducing her to state business.

BELOW

The Dauphin François (1544–60).

By Léonard Limosin, c.1553

CATALOGUE NO. 40

ABOVE, LEFT

Mary of Guise
during her visit
to France in 1550–51.

*Chalk drawing, attributed
to François Clouet, c.1550–51*

CATALOGUE NO. 84

ABOVE, RIGHT

Charles de Guise,
Cardinal of Lorraine
(1524–74).

*Enamel by Léonard
Limosin, c.1557*

CATALOGUE NO. 6

RIGHT

The earliest known
surviving letter of
Mary, Queen of Scots,
written to Mary of Guise
from France, c.1550

CATALOGUE NO. 8

When she was old enough, Mary was able to reply in person and their correspondence flourished. Her French relatives always kept a close eye on her too. Her grandfather, the Duke of Guise, had died in 1550, but she was close to her grandmother, that formidable matriarch Antoinette, Dowager Duchess of Guise, and to one of her uncles in particular, the cultivated, intellectual Charles, Cardinal of Lorraine, who in many ways acted as a surrogate father to her. His enamelled portrait by Limosin gives us a glimpse of this ambitious ecclesiastic.

Although Mary's future seemed secure, the Guises worried constantly that the planned marriage with the Dauphin might never take place. Royal brides in the past had been rejected and sent home before their weddings when political alliances had fallen through or some better candidate had appeared on the scene. Young Mary's marriage would bring the Guise family greatly enhanced power and influence once it was accomplished, and so they constantly emphasised to her, as well as to everyone else, that she was not merely a foreign princess but a queen in her own right – indeed, the most eligible bride in Western Europe.

At last, on 24 April 1558, Mary, by now fifteen, and the Dauphin François were triumphantly married at Notre Dame Cathedral in Paris, with elaborate ceremonial. Mary of Guise was not present, as she had intended to be, for increasing Protestant opposition to her policies meant that she did not dare to leave Scotland. No doubt she was told all about the wedding, and a contemporary pamphlet describes the magnificent procession to the cathedral, as well as the bride's appearance. As tall as her Guise uncles by now, Mary, Queen of Scots wore a white dress with an amazingly long train, a diamond necklace and a gold crown set with jewels. Balls, banquets and masques provided lavish entertainment for several days afterwards. It was probably about this time that the leading court artist, François Clouet, painted a fine, watercolour miniature of Mary in a carnation-coloured gown, with her auburn hair pinned up and a long rope of pearls round her neck (see page 12). She places a ring on the fourth finger of her right hand, an accepted reference to a Roman Catholic marriage. This is probably the miniature that she sent to Elizabeth I some time later, and it is still in the Royal Collection.

Henri II must have been well satisfied that his plans were advancing; almost three weeks before the wedding, on 4 April, Mary had signed a series of very secret documents. The first, a deed of gift, said that because the French kings had always protected and maintained

Scotland against the English, they were to inherit the Scottish kingdom were Mary to die childless. They would also inherit her claim to the throne of England. In the second document, Mary promised that if she did die without an heir, the French king should have all the Scottish crown revenues until he was paid back the huge sums of money he had spent on sending military help to the Scots and bringing up and educating Mary. Thirdly, both she and the Dauphin gave assurances that these promises were legally valid and could not be cancelled by any agreements she had made in the past, or would make in the future.

Mary was fifteen when she signed the documents, and she must have been well aware of what she was doing. Diane de Poitiers, Henri's mistress, observing her conversations with the Scottish commissioners sent to attend her wedding, noted that Mary conducted herself not as an inexperienced child, but as a woman of age and of knowledge. Mary would not have thought of the secret clauses as a betrayal of her own kingdom's independence. She had been brought up by both Mary of Guise and Henri II to believe that a peaceful settlement between the warring Scots, English and French could only be brought about by uniting the three kingdoms under a single monarch. She probably regarded the secret documents as safeguards for Scotland's future against the English threat, and of course as a young bride on the point of marrying, she would almost certainly have believed that she would be the mother of a large family.

On 17 November that same year, Henry VIII's daughter, Elizabeth, inherited the English throne. Her Protestant mother had been his second wife, Anne Boleyn, but Elizabeth had been born when his divorced first wife, the Roman Catholic Catherine of Aragon, was still alive. As a result, Catholics considered Elizabeth to be illegitimate and therefore unable to inherit the crown. Seizing his opportunity, Henri II announced that his daughter-in-law, Mary, Queen of Scots, was the

LEFT

*Queen Elizabeth I
of England* (1533–1603).

*Artist unknown,
painted c.1600*

CATALOGUE NO. 186

rightful Queen of England. Shortly afterwards, Mary's royal canopy, banners and silver plate all appeared with a new coat of arms on them, quartering the arms of England with those of Scotland and France. Henri II did not have long, however, to promote his scheme, for on 10 July 1559 he died as a result of a fatal injury suffered during a tournament, and the Dauphin and Mary became King and Queen of France.

François was crowned at Rheims on 18 September 1559, but although Mary was there she required no coronation for she was already an anointed queen. Young though she was, she had already shown considerable poise, composure and strength of character as she supported her distraught mother-in-law at audiences where foreign emissaries and others came to offer their condolences. She herself had been close to Henri II, but the following year she suffered an even more poignant bereavement. On 11 June 1560 Mary of Guise died in Edinburgh Castle, worn out by her struggle to keep Scotland as a Roman Catholic nation and the ally of France. At first no one knew how to

ABOVE

A cup, or tazza,
decorated with the Royal
Arms of Scotland.

*By Jean de Court
(called Vigier), 1556*

CATALOGUE NO. 46

tell Mary, and when the news was finally broken to her she was inconsolable. 'She loved her mother incredibly, much more than daughters usually love their mothers,' the Venetian ambassador reported. Less than six months after that, on 5 December 1560, three days before her eighteenth birthday, her husband François II died of an ear infection.

Mary was heartbroken. She may not have been romantically in love with François, but he had been her dear friend since early childhood, he had grown into a tall and reasonably handsome young man, and all her hopes for the future would have been centred on him. In spite of her distress, her Guise uncles lost no time in telling her that she must marry again, as quickly as possible. With the death of her husband, she had become Queen Dowager and, as such, she was relegated to a secondary position. François's younger brother, Charles IX, was now King of France and his mother, Catherine de Medici, would rule the country for him as Regent. It was no secret that Catherine saw the Guise family as rivals rather than as faithful subjects. If their need for power were to be satisfied, Mary must find a royal husband of the first rank. Don Carlos, the unmarried heir to the Spanish throne, seemed to be the obvious candidate.

Mary herself was happy with the idea, and the English ambassador at the French court reported that, in his opinion, her greatest concern was the continuation of her honour. She would take a husband who

LEFT

Mary, Queen of Scots
in outdoor attire.

*Artist unknown,
c.1560–92*

CATALOGUE NO. 122

would 'uphold her to be great', rather than one to whom she was physically attracted. She was, he told Elizabeth, 'both of great wisdom for her years, modesty, and also of great judgment in the wise handling of herself and her matters'. However, King Philip II of Spain was himself married to a French princess and had no need for a second French alliance. Apart from that, the French princess in question was Elisabeth, the daughter of Henri II and Catherine de Medici. Catherine had no desire for Mary to go to Spain where, with her striking appearance and charm, she was all too likely to overshadow the young queen.

During these months, the leading French poet, Pierre de Ronsard, saw Mary, Queen of Scots walking in the park at Fontainebleau and composed a poem describing her in her white mourning clothes, her long veils billowing like sails in the wind. She sat again for Clouet, who drew her in that attire and she sent a painted version of his drawing to

her rival, Elizabeth, in an attempt to reassure her that she wanted only friendship. The following spring, Mary visited her Guise relatives in Lorraine, not so much in search of advice but to tell them of a momentous decision that she had taken. She was Queen of Scots and she would return to Scotland. From there, she would have far greater freedom to carry out her ambitions for the Spanish marriage, and she could work towards being recognised as the heir to the English throne. To what extent her uncles may or may not have influenced this decision is not known, but her other friends were horrified when she told them what she intended to do. Just two months after the death of Mary of Guise, the Scottish Parliament had passed a series of laws making Scotland an officially Protestant country, with England replacing France as its natural ally. No Roman Catholic monarch, least of all a woman, would be safe to set foot in Scotland unless she went at the head of an army.

Mary ignored their advice and held meetings with both Roman Catholic and Protestant emissaries from Scotland. She rejected the invitation of the Roman Catholic representative, John Leslie, Bishop of Ross, who would have had her return in order to plunge the country into civil war; but she listened to the Protestant envoy, her half-brother Lord James Stewart, later Earl of Moray, whom she had known when she was a small child. She would have been well aware that he had converted to Protestantism and that people suspected him of being eager to rule Scotland himself, for as her father's son he would have been King of Scots had he not been illegitimate. However, ties of kinship mattered to Mary and she found that she could talk to him. At the end of five days of conversations, they agreed that she would return to rule Scotland in person and that she would respect the Protestant settlement, provided that she was able to attend Mass in her own royal chapel. That being decided, Mary went to Paris to make the arrangements for her voyage.

On 14 August 1561, Mary sailed from Calais. The Cardinal of Lorraine saw her off, urging her at the last moment to leave her glittering collection of jewels with him. She replied with affectionate amusement that if he were willing to trust her to the seas, surely her valuables would be safe too. Her great white galley was captained by Nicholas de Villegagnon, who had brought her to France thirteen years earlier. Three of her younger uncles sailed with her as a temporary escort, and so did the famous maids-of-honour, the Four Maries. Accompanying them was another galley for the rest of the royal servants, and twelve or so merchant ships carrying the Queen's furniture and furnishings,

OPPOSITE PAGE

Mary, Queen of Scots,
in white mourning.

By François Clouet,
c.1560–61

CATALOGUE NO. 11

her clothing, gold and silver plate, her paintings and a hundred horses and mules. Among her most personal items was a precious relic in the form of a double holy thorn given to her by Henri II and believed to have come from Christ's crown of thorns. This had been purchased by Henri's Crusading ancestor, Louis IX. As the French coast receded into the distance, Mary wept, exclaiming over and over, 'Adieu, France. I think I shall never see your shores again'.

The royal convoy sailed into Leith harbour on a foggy August morning, and in the days that followed Mary received a surprisingly enthusiastic welcome. The Scots were delighted to have their monarch back again, and they must have been deeply impressed with her appearance. She was still wearing mourning clothes, but she was a regal figure; and in December, a year after her husband's death, she was able to put aside her widow's garments and array herself as a monarch should. Two months later, one of her French servants, Servais de Condé, made a long and detailed inventory of her clothing. She had fifty-nine dresses, two of them made of cloth of gold. Three were of cloth of silver and twenty-one were black, but they were far from being sombre. Black was the height of fashion, and some were trimmed with gold cord and embroidered with bands of gold thread, while others were sewn with silver braid and fringes. There were white, crimson, yellow, blue, orange, grey and green dresses, and one in carnation colour, perhaps the dress that Mary had worn in the Clouet miniature. A white dress was decorated with artificial roses and little silver balls, and a blue satin dress was sewn all over with silver palms, symbolising victory.

There is no doubt that the Queen was using her appearance to emphasise her status, and her splendid jewellery was also deployed to great effect. She had inherited diamond, ruby and emerald rings from her father, along with diamond and pearl buttons and several jewelled brooches, but the most opulent jewels had been given to her by her French relatives. She had sixteen great necklaces set with diamonds, rubies, sapphires and emeralds, some of them with matching rings, bracelets and belts, not to mention the long ropes of pearls for which she was famous. One of them had no fewer than five hundred and thirty pearls, and in addition she had items set with semi-precious stones, and at least two rosaries consisting of the gold filigree beads known as paternoster beads. Each bead was in two halves, so that

it could be unscrewed and a ball of perfumed musk placed inside.

None of Mary's garments has survived, and very little of her jewellery. Those pieces that do exist are items which have been treasured throughout the centuries because they are traditionally said to have been gifts she gave at different times. There is the delicate enamelled necklace, believed to have been presented to Mary Seton; the beautiful sapphire ring sent to Châtelherault's son, Lord John Hamilton; the string of paternoster beads apparently given to her gentlewoman Gilles Mowbray; and possibly a series of decorative lockets, one set with a cameo of herself. For the most part, however, we have to rely on painted and written descriptions for evidence of her finery and her eagerness to dress in a sumptuous fashion. Her father and her grandfather had been at the centre of glittering and sophisticated royal courts, but in the long years of struggle during her mother's regency, a large proportion of crown revenues had been put to military purposes, royal jewels had been pawned, entertainments had ceased and furnishings had grown shabby. The newly-returned Queen was determined to restore court life and the prestige of the monarchy.

As a ruler Mary was surprisingly successful at first. She listened to the advice of the Earl of Moray and William Maitland of Lethington, known to some as 'Scotland's Machiavelli' because of his cunning political manoeuvring. She attended meetings of her Privy Council, patiently bringing her needlework to occupy her hands while she listened to the members arguing interminably. She struggled with the religious situation, regularly attending Mass and sometimes even trying to placate the fiercely critical Reformer, John Knox. She continued her studies of the classics by reading Greek each morning with George Buchanan, the famous neo-classical scholar and poet. She did her best to calm the in-fighting of her ruthless nobles and she deliberately continued, and organised, the masques and entertainments that had for so long been a feature of the Scottish court.

Accustomed as she was to such spectacles, Mary lost no time in reintroducing them to Scotland, persuading George Buchanan to write the words. The masques infuriated John Knox, who saw them only as a wicked and extravagant waste of time. There is no doubt that Mary loved the dancing and dressing up, but there was more to these events than frivolous amusement. Their chosen themes were part of the Queen's attempts not only to reconcile her warring nobles, but to win the friendship of Elizabeth, the participants portraying gods, goddesses and personifications of amity, virginity and marriage. Mary had

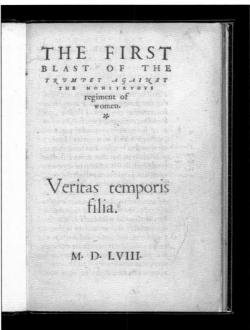

THE FIRST
BLAST OF THE
*TRVMPET AGAINST
THE MONSTRVOVS*
regiment of
women.

Veritas temporis
filia.

M· D· LVIII·

determinedly set out on a policy of conciliating Elizabeth with the aim of being recognised as her heir. This was not an entirely cynical move. Whatever the differences between them, she felt an innate sense of kinship with her rival. As she pointed out, they were, after all, sister monarchs, two queens ruling in the same small island. She corresponded with Elizabeth herself, in the most courteous, friendly terms, sending her small gifts and urging her to arrange an occasion when they could meet face to face. Despite the fictitious scene in Schiller's famous play, *Mary Stuart*, and to Mary's bitter disappointment, the desired encounter never did take place, for Elizabeth's advisers repeatedly postponed and finally cancelled all the plans for it.

As time went by, another problem complicated the relationship between the two queens. Mary needed to secure her own succession, but where was she to find a husband? Her hopes of marrying Don Carlos were fading away and it was not only a dilemma because there were few suitable bridegrooms of her own rank. Her advisers were very conscious that women were subject to the authority of their husbands, and if she became the wife of a Catholic monarch then he would surely transform Scotland once more into a Roman Catholic state. Elizabeth had already witnessed the results when her half-sister, Mary Tudor, intensified her persecution of Protestants after her marriage to Philip II of Spain. Not only was Elizabeth resolved to stay single herself, but she was determined that Mary should not gain the support of a consort who was England's enemy. So she dangled a series of candidates before Mary, whisking them away again before any serious negotiations could take place. When Elizabeth finally suggested Robert Dudley, Earl of Leicester, as a possibility, even the cynical diplomats were shocked; he was widely believed to be Elizabeth's lover. At that, Mary abandoned her attempts to placate the English Queen and turned her thoughts to someone else altogether – her own first cousin, Henry, Lord Darnley.

OPPOSITE, ABOVE LEFT

John Knox (c.1514–72),
the leading Scottish Reformer.

*Artist unknown,
after Adrian Vanson, 1580*

CATALOGUE NO. 61

OPPOSITE, ABOVE RIGHT

*First Blast of the Trumpet
against the Monstrous
Regiment of Women.*

By John Knox, 1558

CATALOGUE NO. 62

OPPOSITE, BELOW

*George Buchanan
(1506–82).*

*Artist unknown,
late 16th century*

CATALOGUE NO. 183

CHAPTER II
Death at Kirk o' Field

THE Darnley marriage is usually presented as a passionate romance which went sadly wrong, and to some extent this may have been true, but there were other considerations as well. Darnley was neither a prince nor a king, but he had royal blood. His father was descended from a daughter of James II, King of Scots, and, more to the point, his mother was a granddaughter of Henry VII of England. In England, as in Scotland, the royal family had dwindled away and there were few available heirs, so a marriage to Darnley would nicely strengthen Mary's claim to the English throne.

His mother, the ambitious and devious Margaret Douglas, Countess of Lennox, was very well aware of these relationships. She had been brought up at the court of Henry VIII, and she and her husband, who was exiled from Scotland, made their home in Yorkshire. She ensured that their eldest surviving son received the best possible education. After the death of François II she knew exactly who she wanted Darnley to marry and, when the time came, she kept pointing out his advantages to Mary, who was her niece, telling her how respectful and obedient he would be if he were her husband. He would be a safe choice, with no ambition to make trouble or try to seize power for himself.

At first Mary was not particularly interested. She had met Darnley twice before, when he was sent to the French court with messages from his mother, and she had received him with casual kindness. Now, in his late teens, he was something of a favourite of Elizabeth I, carrying the sword of honour before her on minor ceremonial occasions.

A beautiful likeness of him was painted in 1560 by Levina Teerlinc, the Flemish female miniaturist to the Tudor monarchs. He might have had effeminate features, as one unkind observer remarked, but he was very tall and athletic, one of the few men, indeed, who could match Mary in height. Her thoughts were, however, elsewhere, but Lady Lennox redoubled her efforts and not only sent her niece a number of

Henry Stewart, Lord Darnley
(1545–67) at fourteen years old.

Attributed to
Levina Teerlinc, 1560

CATALOGUE NO. 133

expensive gifts, but managed to persuade Elizabeth I to allow Darnley to travel to Scotland, which his father was visiting. This was a decision that Elizabeth would come to regret.

Darnley made his way to Wemyss Castle, where Mary was staying, and she greeted him graciously, without showing him any particular favour. After she had observed him for a time, and without apparently telling her Guise relatives, she wrote to Philip II of Spain to ask for his opinion of the young man as a suitor. His response, passed on by the Duke of Alba, was that no one could be better than a member of the Lennox family for helping Mary to secure her claims and bring peace to her country. Even Catherine de Medici, for her own reasons, gave her somewhat tepid approval, and though the Cardinal of Lorraine had written off Darnley as nothing more than a pleasant young nincompoop when he had met him in France, Mary now turned to convincing her own lords. The Earl of Moray, who was jealous of Darnley, refused to agree to the scheme and was sent away in disgrace.

It is tempting to think that the famous Lennox Jewel might have been Darnley's gift to Mary at this time, for heart-shaped lockets were usually love tokens. Set with rubies, an emerald and an imitation sapphire which is actually blue glass, it could have been made in Edinburgh. However, no one has fully unravelled the many intriguing designs and inscriptions which decorate it and it is now thought to have been commissioned in London by Lady Lennox to commemorate the death of her husband in 1571. Whatever the circumstances of its creation, it certainly proclaims the family's closeness to the English throne and their future aspirations. Suddenly very conscious of the danger, Elizabeth I bitterly opposed the match.

By this time Mary seems to have decided that she was in love with Darnley. Not only did he appear to be the answer to so many of her problems, but in contrast to her ambitious, ruthless nobles, he seemed to be utterly trustworthy, an engaging ally. Mary had lost all those emotionally closest to her and, apart from anything else, she must have missed the masculine companionship of François II. Here was another young man who could dance with her, and ride out with her, and share her confidences. She even took to dressing up as a man and wandering incognito about the streets with him in the evenings, exhilarated by the fact that no one recognised her. Darnley had brought fun and friendship back into her life, and if he seemed immature at times, that was somehow rather appealing. After all, he was only nineteen, three years

ABOVE

The Darnley or
Lennox Jewel.

*Maker unknown,
c.1571–78*

CATALOGUE NO. 159

younger than she was. On 22 July she created him Duke of Albany, a title usually kept for members of the Scottish royal family, and she gave in to his demands to be declared king after their wedding, despite her difficulty in persuading a majority of her Privy Council to agree. On 29 July, she married him in the royal chapel at the Palace of Holyroodhouse, and celebrated afterwards with the traditional banquets, balls and masques.

At first the marriage seemed to be a success. When the Earl of Moray, displaced as her chief confidant, rebelled against her, she and Darnley rode out together at the head of an army which pursued Moray until he fled across the border into England. However, once the excitement of the so-called Chaseabout Raid was over, it soon became evident that the Scottish nobles were bitterly jealous of 'King Henry', as he was now known. The wretched youth was vain and arrogant, and ordered them about instead of according them the respect they believed to be their natural right. He would have to go, and the best way to accomplish this would be to stir up trouble between him and the Queen.

This was not difficult to do. Darnley was becoming more petulant by the day. His father and other relatives were always telling him that although he was styled 'King Henry', this simply meant that he was the Queen's Consort. It was her duty, they said, to grant him the Crown Matrimonial, which meant that he and Mary would share power equally; and if she died childless, he would rule alone and his children by a subsequent marriage would succeed him. When Mary refused to comply, he was mortally offended and began to complain to everyone that she was not treating him properly.

Pressing ahead with their plan, his false friends began to insinuate that Mary was having an affair with David Rizzio, the secretary for her French correspondence. By the very nature of his task, Rizzio spent long hours in the Queen's company and the nobles were furious that they, her natural advisers, often had to seek access to her by asking the pompous little Italian to arrange an appointment. Mary liked Rizzio and she was kind to him, as she was to all her servants. He had come to Scotland in the suite of the ambassador from Savoy, who suggested that he could make a career for himself at her court. He possessed a fine bass voice and applied successfully to join the Queen's household as one of her singers. He might have been small, ugly and possibly even deformed, but he was quick-witted and amusing and he was soon

ABOVE

King Henry and
Queen Mary silver ryal.

*Minted in
Edinburgh,* 1565

CATALOGUE NO. 138

BELOW

*James, 4th Earl
of Morton* (1516–81).

*Attributed to Arnold
Bronckorst, c.1580*

SCOTTISH NATIONAL
PORTRAIT GALLERY

promoted. As well as poring over her correspondence during the day, he used to play cards with her in the evening. Proud of his position, he strutted about in expensive silks and velvets, and of course that annoyed the courtiers even more. Sir James Melville remembered long afterwards how some of the nobles glared at the little Italian and shouldered him out of the way if they came into the royal chambers and found him there. The Queen realised what was happening and urged Melville to be kind to 'Seigneur David', saying that he was hated without cause. When she heard about the rumours that she and Rizzio were lovers, she laughed them off. It was too ridiculous that anyone should believe these stories.

The gossip about Rizzio's friendship with Mary was particularly damaging when it became known she was pregnant. Was the coming child really Rizzio's, Darnley's friends asked him, making him feel even more insecure. Meanwhile, Mary was quickly becoming disillusioned with her husband. Instead of the supportive companion she had imagined, he was never there when required. A wooden stamp with a copy of his signature had to be devised so that it could be added to documents in his absence, and it was well known that at night he spent hours roaming around Edinburgh, having sexual relationships, so it was said, with both men and women.

Another element in the situation related to the Earl of Moray, Earl of Morton and their friends, who were still in exile in England, though desperate to return. They knew that the Parliament, due to meet in March, would charge them with treason and deprive them of their lands and they needed to stop this happening. Melville begged Mary to prevent trouble by pardoning them in advance, but she brushed aside the suggestion, remarking that although the Scots were great talkers they rarely put their bragging into effect. However, Elizabeth I was sending letters urging her to be lenient towards Moray and Morton, and Mary did initially postpone the meeting of Parliament, only to change her mind and announce that it would assemble in mid-March, as was originally planned.

With that, the rebels hastily finalised their plan. They must at all costs stop Parliament from sitting and they drew both Darnley and his relatives into the conspiracy by promising to obtain the Crown Matrimonial for him. By the middle of February it was known in London that Darnley and his father were actively plotting to obtain the Scottish crown. Rizzio would be murdered and there was a threat to the Queen herself. Mary, however, knew nothing of what was going on. Now five months pregnant, she attended the opening of Parliament on 12 March, and the members agreed that the bill of attainder against Moray would be passed five days later. Two days after that, the conspirators struck.

The Queen was staying at Holyroodhouse and that evening she was having supper privately, in the little room off her bedchamber. There was really no space for anything in the way of furniture, other than a table and chairs. Mary sat at the middle of the table, with her half-sister Jean, Countess of Argyll, at one end and Rizzio at the other. Her half-brother, Lord Robert Stewart, and her Master of the Household, Robert Beaton, were there too, along with Arthur Erskine, the Captain of her Guard, and her French apothecary. The table was lit by a candle and one or two of the domestic servants came and went with plates and food. It was Lent, but because of her pregnancy Mary was permitted to have meat and a sustaining meal was brought in.

They had just begun to eat when there was the sound of footsteps on the private stair which led to Darnley's chambers on the floor below. A tapestry concealing its door was pushed aside, and to everyone's surprise he himself appeared. In uncharacteristically jovial mood, he sat down beside the Queen and put his arm round her waist. They hardly had time to exchange more than a word when there was suddenly a loud commotion on the stair and a startling figure emerged. For the past three months Lord Ruthven had reportedly been on his deathbed, but now he stood there, in full armour, his face a ghastly white, demanding loudly that the Queen send Rizzio from her presence because of his misdeeds.

Aghast, Mary turned towards Darnley to

demand to know what was happening, while Rizzio, terrified, sought refuge, cowering behind her skirt. Mary ordered Ruthven to leave at once or be condemned as a traitor, but he paid no attention. She rose to her feet in dismay, but Darnley seized her in his arms to restrain her. Her attendants meanwhile sprang towards Ruthven, but he drew a pistol and waved them back. At that moment the door from the main staircase burst open and the Earl of Morton's armed men rushed into the room. The table was overturned, the dishes crashing to the floor. Lady Argyll snatched up the candlestick so that the room was not plunged into darkness. Darnley's dagger was then seized from him by his uncle, George Douglas, who lunged over Mary's shoulder and stabbed Rizzio. Another man held a pistol to the Queen's stomach as, plunging their own daggers into their victim, the rest of the conspirators dragged him away. At Darnley's command, they hurled him down the main stair, hauled his body into the porter's lodge, stripped it of its fine garments and threw it across a storage chest.

Mary survived the shocking events of that night and, although she was held prisoner by the assassins, she managed to draw Darnley back to her side. He had been terrified by the violence and now, fearing for his own life, he turned to her for support, pleading that he was only young and that he had been tricked into taking part. The lords had meant to imprison her in Stirling Castle, he blurted out, and then, when her child was born, would have ruled the country on the baby's behalf. Mary reproached him bitterly for having been part of the plan, but she also told him that, as the father of her coming child, she would never abandon him. Her situation was desperate, but although she wept bitterly for Rizzio's death she was resolutely determined to escape. Playing for time, she pretended to be ill and insisted that she needed a midwife. She also managed to communicate with two of her most loyal supporters, the Earl of Huntly and Earl of Bothwell, who were both outside the Palace. They suggested that the Queen should climb out of a window and down a rope-ladder, but that was far too dangerous for there were guards in the chamber below hers.

Then Mary heard that Moray and Morton had arrived back in Scotland and she agreed to see them. Moray came first, and they had an emotional reunion, both of them shedding tears. The following day, he returned with Morton and they knelt and asked her pardon for their rebellion. Mary refused to give it until, she said, they had redeemed themselves by their future behaviour. When Moray launched into a lengthy lecture about the virtues of clemency, Mary replied briskly that, from her earliest days, her subjects had given her plenty of opportunity to practise that particular quality. She then left the room.

In the middle of that same night, Mary and Darnley crept down the small private stair to his apartments, through the passages, past the rooms where her French servants stayed, and out at the back of the Palace to the gate where Arthur Erskine was waiting with horses. Mary rode pillion behind Erskine, while Darnley spurred away, complaining vociferously that they should have been taking his father with them. Five hours later they reached the safety of Dunbar Castle.

Mary's supporters rallied to her side and on 18 March she was able to enter Edinburgh once more. For safety she moved into the Castle, a formidable fortress. There she was reconciled with Moray, and further arranged a reconciliation between him, Bothwell and Huntly. She also made her will, dividing up her valuables between the crown of Scotland and her friends and relatives, and leaving twenty-five items of jewellery to Darnley, including her wedding ring. On 19 June 1566, her healthy son was born in the little room which is now painted with the Royal Coat of Arms and the date of his birth. He would be named James, as his grandfather and predecessors had been.

The Queen's relationship with Darnley remained very strained. While she lay in bed, recovering from her lengthy labour, she sent for him. Before a number of her household, she showed him the baby, telling him that the child was his. 'He is so much your own son,' she added bitterly, 'that I fear it will be the worse for him hereafter.'

There was much public rejoicing at the birth of this male heir, but Mary knew her position had become increasingly vulnerable. In the past, the Scottish nobility had taken advantage of royal minorities to increase their own power and possessions, and she was haunted by the fear that they might indeed try to seize the baby and rule on his behalf. She endeavoured to be in Darnley's company as much as possible, even agreeing to sleep with him once more for she needed to keep his confidence in order to know what he was doing. But during their public appearances together, the two often shocked people with their quarrelling.

In August, Mary took her son to Stirling Castle where, according to tradition, as heir to the throne, he would be brought up under the guardianship of Lord Mar. Meanwhile, matters with her husband were going from bad to worse; he had begun to tell people that he meant to leave Scotland. The Queen, his wife, was not treating him properly, he said, and so he would go to France and live on her jointure revenues

there. As the widow of François II, Mary had a considerable income assigned to her by the terms of her marriage contract. Her reaction to this may be imagined, and her lords were affronted. This would be an incredible insult to the Queen. Her Privy Council even reminded him publicly that he ought to thank God for giving him such a wise and virtuous wife, and Mary took his hand and urged him to tell her if she had ever given him any cause to behave in this way. Darnley could not think up a convincing reply. Instead, when she asked him to travel with her through Teviotdale, where she would dispense justice, he refused to join her and instead remained at home writing long letters to the Pope, to France, to Spain, and to anyone else he could think of, complaining that Mary was not a good Catholic.

The Queen became ill as she rode through the Borders, but when she heard that Lord Bothwell had been gravely injured in a skirmish, she insisted on going to him in his Hermitage Castle. It was twenty-five miles from where she was staying, and riding there and back in one day proved too much for her. She collapsed with an alarming illness, possibly caused by a duodenal ulcer. Convinced she was dying, Mary sent for her lords and told them that her husband must not be allowed to seize the crown. Her son would succeed her and he must be brought up with due care. She realised that he would be raised as a Protestant, but she urged that he be taught to show tolerance to Roman Catholics, just as she had never persecuted Protestants.

Mary lapsed into unconsciousness, but was saved by her French physician. Although she took weeks to recover, she appeared to remain deeply depressed, blaming the stress of Darnley's behaviour for her illness. Mary, however, was always given to a dramatic turn of phrase and, once back in Edinburgh, was often heard to exclaim, 'I would wish to be dead'.

She and her lords now had long discussions about the problem of Darnley. The royal marriage could not be annulled on any pretext, for that would have made Prince James illegitimate. Divorce, however, was a possibility. There were Darnley's affairs with various prostitutes; and evidence of some long-standing adulterous relationship would have been easy enough to concoct. However, even this was no real solution as, under the rules of the Church, divorce did not end a marriage entirely. In the eyes of God a couple remained husband and wife, and so neither was free to re-marry.

The lords no doubt favoured a swift and decisive solution to the problem and, although they did not enter into details, Maitland of

Lethington apparently told Mary that if some method of eliminating Darnley could be found, then Moray was willing to turn a blind eye to whatever was decided. The Queen was horrified. They must do nothing to stain her honour or her conscience, she told them. Their intended victim was not only her husband, but the monarch of a kingdom; she could not countenance an attack on him. Mary had been brought up in the exalted French notion of kingship, and throughout her life she believed that monarchs were set apart, chosen by God to rule their kingdoms.

Jealous of Darnley and infuriated by his behaviour, the lords were not going to pay much attention to Mary's remonstrations. They probably believed that she would be too relieved once Darnley had gone to take any action against them. When their discussions ended, the Queen may have felt reassured that at least her lords were obviously not plotting with Darnley against her, and she turned her attention to a much more pleasant matter. For weeks now she had been planning the baptism of Prince James. His godparents were to be the King of France, Elizabeth I of England, and the Duke of Savoy. They would not, of course, attend in person, but Elizabeth, who was famously careful with her money, surprised everyone by sending the gift of a magnificent gold font set with precious stones for the ceremony.

The only person who was not pleased was Darnley. At one time high in the favour of Elizabeth, he now hated the English Queen because she had opposed his marriage. He leapt to the conclusion that Mary had deliberately selected her as a godparent in order to annoy him, and after another furious quarrel with her he refused to attend the baptism or any of the celebrations.

The Roman Catholic ceremony took place on 7 December in the Chapel Royal of Stirling Castle and was followed by three days of celebration – with banquets, dancing and masques, culminating in a spectacular firework assault on an imitation fort, the participating 'wild highlanders' dressed from head to foot in goatskins. The defenders of the fort repulsed the invaders, thereby conveying the message that the peace and stability brought by the Stewart monarchy had conquered conflict and chaos. The elaborate masque was very much in the French style, and indeed it had been devised by another of Mary's *valets-de-chambre*, Sebastien Pagez. A clever, witty man, Pagez probably came from Lorraine and was generally known as 'Bastien', a favourite diminutive name there. Whatever his origins, he had already produced a number of other masques for celebrations at Mary's court.

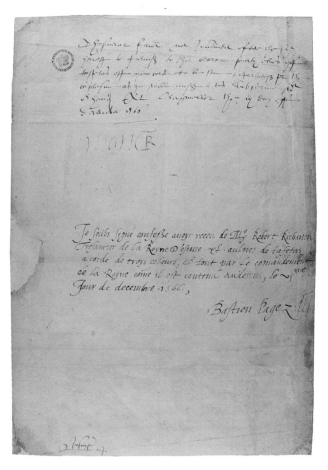

Unable to get anyone to listen to his interminable complaints, Darnley had left Stirling on Christmas Eve, having decided to join his father in Glasgow. That same day he fell seriously ill with a rash and high fever, and when he arrived in Glasgow the doctors diagnosed small-pox. Historians are inclined to believe that, judging by the treatments he was given, he was actually suffering from an advanced case of syphilis. Certainly the Earl of Bothwell thought so, according to an account of events he wrote in later years.

At first the Queen appeared to have considered this a feigned illness, another of her husband's ploys to gain her attention, but when Mary was assured that he really was dangerously ill, she sent a royal physician to attend him.

Explaining that she had injured herself in a fall from her horse, Mary did not ride to Glasgow to see Darnley in person until 20 January, a sensible enough delay when he was thought to be suffering from a highly dangerous infection. But when Mary was shown into her husband's bedchamber, she was met by a pitiful sight. Darnley was lying in bed, a mere shadow of his former self, a taffeta mask concealing the sores on his pretty features. She informed him that she was willing to live with him again as his wife once he had recovered. Indeed, she had brought a horse-litter with her, so that she could take him back to Edinburgh. Darnley was terrified at the thought of being anywhere near the lords with whom he had conspired, for they knew he had deserted them and he was convinced they would try to kill him. Mary assured him of her protection.

But just how genuine was her desire to be reconciled with him? Did she really mean it, seeing it as the only way out of their impossible situation, or was it part of a sinister plan to rid herself of him once and for all?

Whatever her intentions, Darnley agreed to go with her, and at the end of the month they set out for Edinburgh, Mary on horseback, her husband lying in the litter. He would not be taken to Holyroodhouse until he recovered, for the baby Prince was there. Instead, Mary had intended him to stay at Craigmillar Castle, but he was frightened of its keeper, Sir Simon Preston. In the end he was persuaded to occupy a house at Kirk o' Field, which was much nearer to Holyroodhouse and just inside the town wall.

It stood on the site of what is now the University of Edinburgh's Old College, just across narrow College Street from the present-day National Museum of Scotland. The Duke of Châtelherault owned a large mansion at Kirk o' Field, which his illegitimate half-brother, the Archbishop John Hamilton, was currently using, and it formed one side of what was obviously quite a fashionable square, the other three sides being occupied by smaller, gabled houses. Darnley, of course, demanded to be taken to the Hamilton house, but he was told that this was impossible. Instead he was installed in the building known as the Old Provost's Lodging.

Word had been sent ahead of the change of plan, and the house was hastily furnished for his arrival. The first floor bedchamber would be his. It was hung with tapestries which had once belonged to a previous Earl of Huntly, and there was a regal-looking chair covered in purple velvet, several red velvet cushions, a little table, and a bed hung with black. Next to the bed was a bath, because frequent bathing was needed to help Darnley's sores to heal, and the Queen gave orders that a door elsewhere in the house was to be taken from its hinges to serve as a cover for the bath when it was not in use. Always conscious of his status, Darnley protested that the black bed was shabby, and so Mary had a richly-embroidered bed hung with violet-brown velvet curtains, trimmed with gold and silver, brought up for him from Holyroodhouse. The bed had belonged to her mother; Mary had given it to Darnley some months earlier, so he could hardly complain that it was not grand enough for him.

Mary also tried to reassure him about his safety, for he was still very nervous of being attacked by some of his former co-conspirators. She spent a good deal of time with him, encouraging her lords to do likewise, so that his bedchamber was usually crowded with visitors. He was not yet in a fit state for her to sleep with him, but downstairs was another bedchamber, with a yellow and green bed, and there Mary spent the night of the Wednesday and Friday of that first week.

On 9 February, Mary had many things to do. Sebastien Pagez was set to be married that day to one of his colleagues, Christine Hogg, a Scottish chamber-woman in the royal household. That morning, the Queen had given her a wedding present of thirteen and three-quarter ells of black satin to create a wide-sleeved gown lined with velvet, and thirty-two ells of green ribbon for a skirt and hood. At noon, Mary attended the wedding feast, and afterwards she rode up to Kirk o' Field where she intended to spend the night.

During the evening, reportedly between ten and eleven o'clock, someone reminded Mary that she had promised to attend Bastien's wedding masque, and so she prepared to leave. Darnley protested, of course, but she had promised to be there. In fact she had missed most of the masque, but she did arrive in time for the ceremonial bedding of bride and groom, amidst the customary ribald merriment. After that, Mary retired to her own bedchamber. Four hours later she, along with everyone else in the Palace, was aroused by a deafening noise that shook the entire area. Alarmed and confused, she asked her ladies what cannon were firing, thinking that someone had started to besiege the largely unfortified building. But no one knew what was happening. The Earl of Bothwell, who had been spending the night at the Palace after the festivities, quickly took charge. As he was the Sheriff of Edinburgh, he sent messengers to find out what had happened.

All over the town, people had risen from their beds and hurried outside to discover what dreadful disaster had occurred. Those who lived in the small houses at Kirk o' Field stared in disbelief. The Old Provost's Lodging, where Darnley had been staying, had been completely demolished. There was nothing but a huge pile of rubble where it had been. Suddenly they heard a faint cry for help, and there was the tattered figure of one of Darnley's servants, standing on top of the town wall. Realising that there might be other survivors, the bystanders began to dig about frantically in the wreckage, fearing that the Queen herself might have been in the house. It was a bitterly cold night, and pitch dark apart from the light of their lanterns, but eventually they brought out the bodies of two more of Darnley's servants. Presumably news began to filter through that the Queen was safe in Holyroodhouse, but of her husband there was no sign.

Later, as morning came, someone went into the garden beyond the town wall and discovered two corpses. One was that of Lord Darnley, wearing only his nightshirt and lying beneath a tree. A yard or two away was Taylor, his *valet-de-chambre*. Nearby were a chair, a dagger, a coat and a cloak. Some of the eye-witnesses said that these miscellaneous items had been laid out neatly, as though arranged very deliberately. A drawing of the scene, sent to Queen Elizabeth's leading statesman, William Cecil, shows them lying in a row, between the dead men and some trees (see pages 40–41). Beyond that are men on horseback. As was the way with such pictures of the period, several small scenes show the sequence of events.

Here we have an innocent-looking Darnley sitting up in bed saying a prayer before going to sleep, although the words emerging, cartoon-like, from his mouth actually say 'Judge and avenge my cause, O Lord'. There, in a lively depiction of the square, a group of neighbours gaze in shock at the rubble strewn along the entire side where the Old Provost's Lodging had stood. In the right, lower corner of the drawing, a corpse is being buried in a summary fashion beside a nearby church, and to the left, another body is being carried away, watched by a half-circle of bystanders as some armed men hurry forward. This presumably represents Darnley. His corpse was taken into the house next to the rubble and doctors were summoned to examine it, in the presence of some members of the Privy Council. No doubt to their surprise, there was no sign of violence on either his body or the valet's. They must have expected to find terrible injuries as a result of the explosion, but there was nothing, not even any singeing of the hair or blackening of the face. There were no stab wounds or gunshot wounds or signs of beating. The two men must have been either strangled (which could have been expected to leave marks on the neck) or asphyxiated.

When the doctors had completed their examinations, members of the public were allowed in to look at Darnley before his body was placed on a board and carried down to Holyroodhouse.

It was Bothwell who broke the news to the Queen. Badly shaken, Mary gave orders that her husband should be embalmed and then lie in state in the royal chapel. In other circumstances Mary wept easily, but when her lords insisted that she go and look at her dead husband, she stood there in silence, her face expressionless, seemingly in a state of deep shock. Later that week, Darnley was buried by night in her father's vault in the ruined Holyrood Abbey.

The etiquette for royal mourning meant that Mary should have remained in her darkened chamber for forty days, but her doctors were so worried about her health that they persuaded the Queen to leave the Palace at the end of the first week. Entrusting Prince James to the care of her two faithful supporters, the Earl of Bothwell and

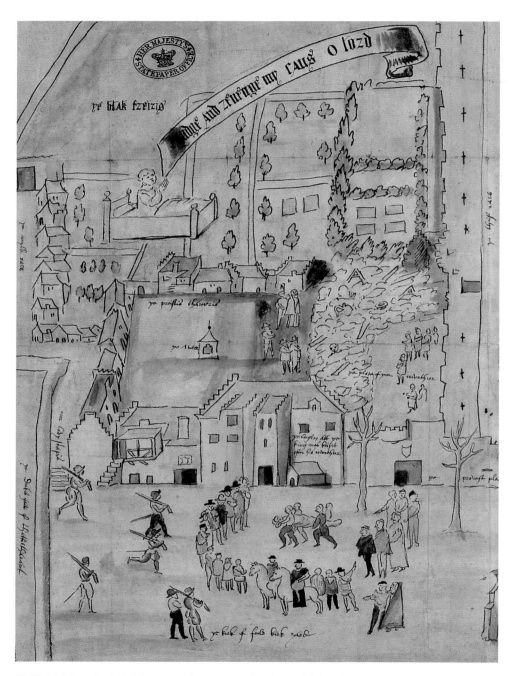

THIS PAGE AND OPPOSITE: *Bird's Eye View of Kirk o' Field* (details), *1567*. CATALOGUE NO. 150

BELOW

A placard representing
Mary, Queen of Scots
and the Earl of Bothwell
as a mermaid and a hare.

Artist unknown, c.1567

CATALOGUE NO. 154

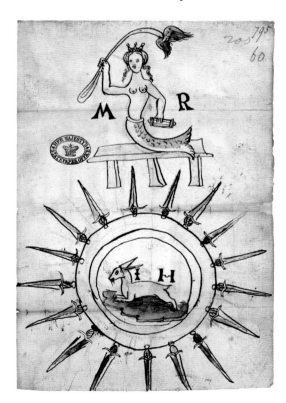

the Earl of Huntly, she travelled along the coast to stay at Lord Seton's house.

Did Mary's reaction to her husband's murder indicate her innocence or guilt? Had she exclaimed to her lords at Craigmillar Castle, with characteristic passion, 'Yes! Yes! You must free me from him', and then been horrified when they took her at her word? It is impossible to say, but, as Professor John Guy has remarked, not one piece of uncontaminated evidence has ever been found to suggest that Mary knew of the plot. Her enemies would accuse her of having deliberately lured Darnley to Kirk o' Field in the knowledge that he was to die there, while her dwindling number of friends protested that her journey to Glasgow had been undertaken because she really had decided to reconcile with him and knew nothing of what was planned.

Official investigations into the tragedy led only to further confusion. Both Moray and Maitland had been absent from Edinburgh on that fateful night, presumably because they knew what was coming. Some of the lesser men involved claimed that the gunpowder for the explosion had been stored in the house next door to the Old Provost's Lodging and that they had seen Bothwell rushing about, supervising operations. Indeed, once the fuse was lit, he had stepped forward in his impatience to see it burn, and was dragged back in the nick of time by one of his companions. A couple of women who lived at Kirk o' Field told the ambassador from Savoy, the Marquis of Moretta, that although they had observed thirteen men hurrying along the lane behind the Old Provost's Lodging, only eleven had returned. They also alleged that they had heard Darnley screaming for mercy. As for Mary herself, she was highly indignant when she heard the rumours that Bothwell, her faithful ally, had been the principal murderer, and in her own correspondence she always expressed the conviction that she too had been an intended victim that night at Kirk o' Field.

Others had a very different perception of events. The very day after Mary left Edinburgh, placards began to appear, accusing Bothwell of being the murderer, and by 1 March there was a new accusation. This came in the form of a drawing of a hare, an animal which featured on Bothwell's family crest, in a circle of swords, with a mermaid, the symbol for a prostitute, wearing a crown. The message was all too clear. Mary had been Bothwell's lover, and had known what he was going to do in advance. She had been complicit in the assassination. One of the placards was sent to William Cecil and his colleagues in London as evidence of her guilt, and it is preserved in The National Archives at Kew.

Historians at one time believed that there were several plots involved in the events at Kirk o' Field, with the different groups rushing about in a disorganised fashion. The general consensus now is that there was one single conspiracy, with Bothwell's men laying the gunpowder and some of Morton's men stationed at the back of the Old Provost's Lodging in case something went wrong and the intended victim did not die in the explosion. Given the condition of the bodies of Darnley and his valet, it seems that something must have alarmed them and they had managed to get out of the building before it was blown to pieces. The chair found in the garden would have been used in their escape to lower Darnley from his first floor bedchamber, and the garments were no doubt intended for him to put on as he hid outside in the bitter cold of that February night.

The scale of the explosion can be explained as an effort to ensure that no incriminating evidence survived, or simply as another example of Bothwell's reckless determination. Quite why the murderers did not save themselves a lot of trouble by slipping poison into Darnley's drink is another unanswered question, but then subtlety was never their strong point.

In 2010 the site of Kirk o' Field was excavated because the University of Edinburgh was about to landscape its Old Quadrangle. The archaeologists did not expect to find anything which would throw more light on the murder at Kirk o' Field, and so it proved to be; there had been too many alterations when the Old College was built in the late eighteenth century. Although they did come upon some stonework from the Hamilton mansion (built in 1552 for the Duke of Châtelherault), and some pieces of sixteenth-century pottery, there was nothing further to help solve the enduring mystery of Darnley's death.

ABOVE

Earthenware fragments, found during a recent archaeological dig at Kirk o' Field.

French, 16th century

CATALOGUE NO. 151

CHAPTER III
The Disastrous Marriage

HAD Mary acted immediately, she could possibly have saved
her reputation, but she failed to summon the suspects before
Parliament and so it was left to Darnley's devastated father,
the Earl of Lennox, to accuse Bothwell of the murder. The date for the
trial was fixed, and Lennox set out for Edinburgh with an army of three
thousand men. When he arrived at Linlithgow he was informed that he
could bring only a retinue of six people with him. Fearing for his life,
he returned home. Bothwell was finally tried on 12 April 1567, but the
town was packed with his supporters and he was swiftly acquitted. Four
days later, Mary opened Parliament, Bothwell walking in the procession carrying the royal sceptre.

Basking in the Queen's favour, Bothwell decided that he
would marry her. The fact that he already had a wife did not
deter him. Mary herself had arranged his marriage to the
wealthy Lady Jean Gordon the previous year, in order to
solve his financial problems. He was a Protestant, she came
from a staunchly Catholic family and was in love with someone else, but that did not matter in a world where marriage
choice was very often governed by the acquisition of property.
Husband and wife both raised actions for divorce and Bothwell
is said to have proposed to the Queen on several occasions that
spring. She refused him, but he persisted. He also gathered together
a group of leading lords and bishops, and persuaded or bullied them
into signing a document saying that he was innocent of any part in the
Darnley murder and recommending him as a husband for the Queen.

Mary knew perfectly well that she was liable to ruin herself if she
married Bothwell, and friends and relatives in France and elsewhere
lost no time in writing to warn her against taking him as her husband. Even so, she did not dismiss the idea. If we believe that Mary
was already his sexual partner and his accomplice in murder, then no

ABOVE

James Hepburn,
4th Earl of Bothwell
(c.1535–78).

Artist unknown, 1566

CATALOGUE NO. 153

further explanation need be sought, but her Dominican confessor solemnly swore to the Spanish ambassador in London that until the Bothwell marriage became an issue, he had never seen a woman of greater courage, virtue and uprightness. She genuinely seems to have feared that she and her little son were in mortal danger and that what she needed above all else was a strong and influential protector. How could she go on otherwise? Her secretary had been brutally killed in her very presence – and now her unsatisfactory husband had been murdered.

Mary had lengthy discussions with Maitland of Lethington during these weeks. In January he had married Mary Fleming, who was her cousin and one of her Four Maries, and she evidently thought that she could trust him. Perhaps it was he who came up with the solution that the Bothwell marriage could take place if it seemed that it had been forced upon her.

On 20 April 1567, Mary went to Stirling to visit Prince James. On the way back, her cavalcade was intercepted by Bothwell with a small army. He declared that he had come to escort her to Dunbar Castle for safety, because her life was in danger. She offered no resistance and rode there with her retinue. Sir James Melville was one of her companions, and he later said that when they arrived Bothwell raped her. She herself would remark that although his actions were rough, his words were gentle. After that, the only way to save her honour was to marry him. It was her greatest mistake.

The wedding took place on 15 May 1567, in the Great Hall at Holyroodhouse, where the Privy Council usually met. It was a Protestant service and there were no celebrations. That afternoon the Queen wept and assured John Leslie, Bishop of Ross, that she already regretted it had not been a Roman Catholic ceremony, adding that she would never abandon the Catholic Church. He believed her, and would be for the most part her ally in the years ahead. Her lords, of course, far from supporting the marriage which many of them had recommended, were now bitterly jealous of Bothwell. Led by Morton, they decided on military opposition. Mary in turn gathered together her forces and the two armies met at Carberry Hill, near Musselburgh, on 15 June. The lords carried with them a huge white banner with a design closely resembling one of the scenes on the Kirk o' Field drawing. The murdered Darnley lay beneath his tree, and this time Prince James knelt at his feet, exclaiming, 'Judge and revenge my cause, O Lord'.

The two armies confronted each other throughout that day, and

ABOVE

A sketch of a banner
used by the Lords at
Carberry Hill, 1567.

CATALOGUE NO. 155

Bothwell would have rushed down the hill to engage in single combat, if Mary had not restrained him. As evening came, however, and her forces began to drift away, she told him to leave. There would have to be a proper investigation into the Darnley murder, she said. If he were found innocent, she would live again as his wife; but if he were guilty, she would do everything she could to free herself from the marriage. He went, eventually seeking refuge in Scandinavia, only to spend the rest of his life in a Danish prison.

Mary rode down the hill and surrendered to Sir William Kirkcaldy of Grange. The lords escorted her back to Edinburgh, an exhausted and dishevelled prisoner, with crowds of onlookers hurling insults. The following night she was taken briefly to Holyroodhouse and then, with only two chamber-women for company, to Lochleven Castle, on a small lake near Kinross. In the castle, which belonged to the Earl of Moray's half-brother, Sir William Douglas, Mary was held captive.

The Queen must have known or suspected that she was pregnant at this time, and on about 23 July she miscarried twins. The following day, lying in bed, weak from loss of blood, she was forced by Lord Lindsay to sign a document abdicating in favour of her son, Prince James. Queen Elizabeth had sent Sir Nicholas Throckmorton to Scotland to find out what was happening, and though he had been unable to see Mary he had managed to smuggle in a message urging her to do everything she could to save her own life. She could agree to anything, he had told her, for promises extracted under duress had no force in law, and that was her belief also. Five days after that, thirteen-month-old Prince James was crowned in the now Protestant Chapel Royal at Stirling Castle. John Knox preached the sermon.

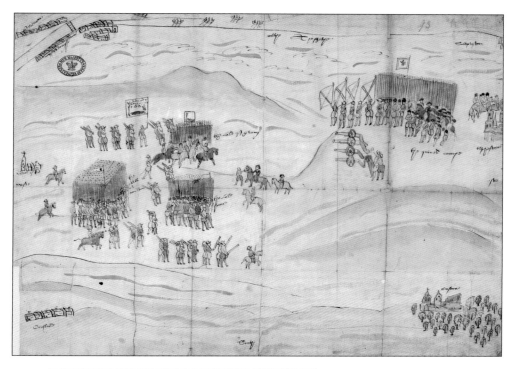

BELOW

*The Memorial of
Lord Darnley.*

*By Livinus
de Vogelaare, 1567*

CATALOGUE NO. 158

Mary never did accept the legality of her abdication and quarrelled bitterly with Moray when he arrived back in Scotland and came to see her. He was publicly proclaimed Regent a few days later, telling people that Mary had given her approval, which of course she had not. He then took possession of her priceless collection of jewels, giving some to his wife and selling the rest. Elizabeth I and Catherine de Medici engaged in a bidding war to purchase Mary's famous pearls, and it was Elizabeth who secured them.

Meanwhile, in London, the sorrowing Countess of Lennox commissioned from the leading Flemish artist, Livinus de Vogelaare, a very large vengeance painting. In an imaginary ecclesiastical interior, in front of the imaginary tomb of Lord Darnley, featuring his life-like effigy wearing gilded armour, the kneeling figures of a small King James, the Earl and Countess of Lennox and their younger son Charles demand – in Latin – vengeance for his death. Placards on the walls emphasise the message and implicate Queen Mary. A vignette on the lower left shows the scene at Carberry Hill. It is surprising, and perhaps not without significance, that the Countess of Lennox was eventually reconciled with Mary, declaring that she believed her account of events.

That lay in the future, however, and from the moment that she signed the abdication papers, Mary was desperate to regain her freedom and her throne. She wrote to Catherine de Medici begging for military assistance, and to Elizabeth – all to no purpose.

The months went by, and on 25 March 1568 Mary disguised herself as one of the washerwomen who came over from the shore to Lochleven Castle, in an attempt to get away. She was spotted when the boatman noticed her smooth white hands and he returned her to the island, although he did not tell her captors. The failure to escape simply made Mary more determined than ever.

On 2 May she tried again and this time she was successful. Wearing an old red kirtle beneath her cloak, she managed to conceal herself under the seat of a boat and was rowed across the loch, where two of her supporters were waiting with horses purloined from Sir William Douglas's own stable. They quickly rode away together, to join Lord Seton, who took Mary to his castle of Niddry, near Winchburgh.

After resting there, Mary rode west to Hamilton, where Archbishop Hamilton was waiting to greet her. Now that they knew she was free, her supporters were arriving from all over the country. Just six days after her escape, nine earls, nine bishops, eighteen lords and many others signed a document swearing loyalty to her and promising assistance.

The Earl of Moray was in Glasgow when, to his astonishment, he heard of Mary's escape, and he hastened to gather his own army. On 13 May the two forces met at the village of Langside, near Glasgow. Although smaller, Moray's army was much more experienced, and when Mary's general, her brother-in-law the Earl of Argyll, suffered what may have been an epileptic seizure at the very start, her soldiers were left without a leader. Mary never lacked courage. Watching from a nearby hill, she saw that Moray's men had the upper hand and, according to a report sent to Catherine de Medici, she rode down into the thick of the battle, ready to lead her army herself. However, when she saw that her own men were in disarray, quarrelling with each other, she knew that all was lost. For the first time in her life, she turned and fled.

Mary was joined by Lord Herries and a small group of loyal followers. She had sometimes in the past disguised herself as a man for high-spirited fun, but now she put on a man's clothes out of fear and desperation, cutting short her long auburn hair. With no woman to attend her, she and her friends rode south for ninety-two miles without stopping. She described the nightmare journey a month later in a letter to her uncle, the Cardinal of Lorraine, recalling that for the first three

RIGHT

The Herries Book of
Hours, believed to have
been left by Mary, Queen
of Scots at Terregles on her
last night in Scotland.

Late 16th century

CATALOGUE NO. 172

nights they had slept on the ground and had only oatmeal and sour milk for sustenance. Reaching the safety of Terregles Castle, they argued bitterly about what to do next. When Mary announced that she would go to England to seek the help of Queen Elizabeth, the others were horrified. She insisted that Elizabeth would be sure to give her the military assistance she required to regain her throne for, whatever the differences between them, they were sister queens. Urgently the others warned her against doing this, advising Mary that she should go to France. No English monarch could be trusted, they said, reminding her that her own ancestor, James I, had been held captive in England for years and her father had wisely declined to meet his uncle Henry VIII in York for fear of the same thing happening to him. But Mary would not listen. 'I commanded my best friends to permit me to have my own way,' she said afterwards, and she vowed that by the end of August she would be back in Scotland at the head of an army. Next morning, disguising herself this time as an ordinary woman, Mary went down to the River Solway and crossed into England.

The group spent that night in Workington Hall, which was owned by a friend of Lord Herries, after which Mary expected to set out at once for London. She was dismayed when the Deputy Governor of Carlisle arrived the next morning with several hundred horsemen and announced that, instead, he was escorting her to Carlisle Castle. Mary tried to reassure her friends by saying that, naturally, there would be some delay before she could set out for the capital, but as the days and weeks went by, she came to realise the dreadful truth. She was a prisoner.

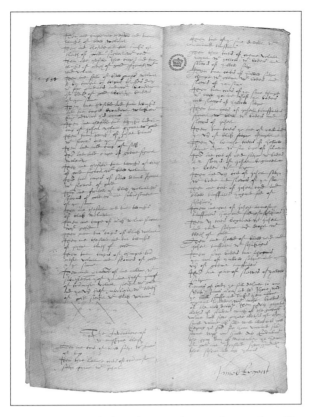

LEFT

An inventory of books,
ornaments and masquing
clothes left behind by
Mary, Queen of Scots
when she fled to England,

Dated to 1569

CATALOGUE NO. 100

BELOW

*William Cecil,
1st Baron Burghley
(1520–98).*

Artist unknown, c.1585

CATALOGUE NO. 187

Mary's arrival on English soil created an embarrassing dilemma for Elizabeth and her advisers, and indeed it was more than that. It was a danger to the English Queen's life and to the stability of her country. There were Roman Catholics in England, as well as abroad, who would seize upon any opportunity to depose her and replace her with the Catholic Queen of Scots. Mary had not been entirely mistaken in Elizabeth's reaction, for Elizabeth was indeed averse to the idea of rebellion against any monarch, including Mary. However, her own safety was paramount, as her staunchly Protestant statesmen, led by William Cecil, never failed to remind her. The initial report they received about Mary merely emphasised the problem. Elizabeth had dispatched Sir Francis Knollys, a Puritan gentleman, to go and inspect the Queen of Scots. His description clearly echoed his surprise. 'This lady and princess is a notable woman,' he said. She was friendly, talkative and ready to expose herself to all perils in order to wreak vengeance on her enemies. As others had noticed before, her honour

53

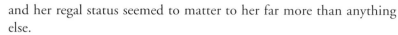

BELOW

The Lennoxlove Casket.

15th century

CATALOGUE NO. 167

and her regal status seemed to matter to her far more than anything else.

Still waiting eagerly to be told that she could now come to London, Mary was shocked when, on 8 June, a messenger came from the English Queen saying that she could not possibly receive the Queen of Scots until she was cleared of the accusations against her. Elizabeth proceeded to set up an official enquiry to examine Mary's complaints that her subjects had unjustly rebelled against her, and the Earl of Moray's assertions that she had committed adultery and murder. What angered Mary most was the implication that she somehow came under Queen Elizabeth's jurisdiction. That was completely wrong, Mary declared, because she herself was an independent sovereign, accountable to no one but God alone.

The enquiry opened in York on 4 October 1568. Mary was not permitted to attend in person, but was allowed to send commissioners to put her case. English commissioners led by Thomas, 4th Duke of Norfolk, would judge whether or not she should be restored to her throne. Moray had not only employed George Buchanan to compile a virulent set of accusations against Mary, but he made much of the fact that he was bringing with him a silver casket containing papers that clearly proved his half-sister's guilt. The casket had been discovered in the possession of one of Bothwell's servants, George Dalgleish, and had been given to the Earl of Morton. When unlocked, it was found to contain twelve poems, two marriage contracts and, most importantly, eight love letters said to have been written by Mary to Bothwell. One, sent from Glasgow when she was visiting her sick husband, was particularly incriminating, for in it we seem to hear her authentic voice as she expresses her distaste for Darnley, her intention to lure him back to Edinburgh, and her passion for Bothwell.

Despite their apparently damning content, the Duke of Norfolk made it known that he was perfectly willing to marry Mary if that would solve the problem of what to do with her, and the other English commissioners also remained very doubtful about the so-called evidence. The discussions dragged on for weeks until, in an attempt to bring them to a conclusion, they were moved to Westminster. On 7 December 1568, Moray for the first time produced the Casket Letters in public. The opinion of historians today is that these documents were a concoction – a mixture of fragments of genuine letters from Mary, pieces of messages to Bothwell from one of his mistresses, and possibly additional forgeries. Unfortunately, they cannot be subjected to the scrutiny of modern scientific techniques for they have long since disappeared.

The enquiry finally ended at the beginning of January 1569 with an inconclusive verdict. Nothing had been proved against either Mary or Moray, but she remained a prisoner, while he returned to Scotland, taking with him the silver casket and its contents, which he gave back to Morton. They were later passed to the Earl of Gowrie, but after his execution in 1584 both casket and letters vanished.

Years passed, and nothing more was heard of the casket and letters until, sometime after 1632, 'a papist' arrived to see the Marchioness of Douglas, who was also a Roman Catholic, and offered to sell her the famous casket, which was now empty. We can only assume that the letters had long since been destroyed. The Marchioness bought it and, after her death in 1674, most of her valuables were sold. The casket, the work of a fifteenth-century French silversmith, was purchased by her daughter-in-law, Anne, 3rd Duchess of Hamilton. At some point someone, presumably her mother-in-law, had ordered the Douglas coat of arms to be engraved on it, but now, at her husband's request, Duchess Anne had this replaced with the Hamilton arms. On 10 August 1705, when she drew up a list of the silver plate she intended to bequeath to her eldest son, James, 4th Duke of Hamilton, included among the dishes, chocolate pot and the cutlery was 'a gilded silver box which was Queen Mary's of Scotland'. It has remained in the possession of the Duchess's descendants ever since.

Had Mary been a nondescript, timid little woman, she could perhaps have been safely married off to some loyal English nobleman and forgotten about, but she was a force to be reckoned with, passionate, eloquent and determined, and so captivity must be her fate. Mary was not shut up in a prison cell, of course. She was, in effect, kept under house arrest. She was allowed to have her own household of a fluctuating number of attendants, including Mary Seton of the Four Maries, but her windows had gratings on them, soldiers guarded her antechambers, and on the occasions when she was allowed to take some

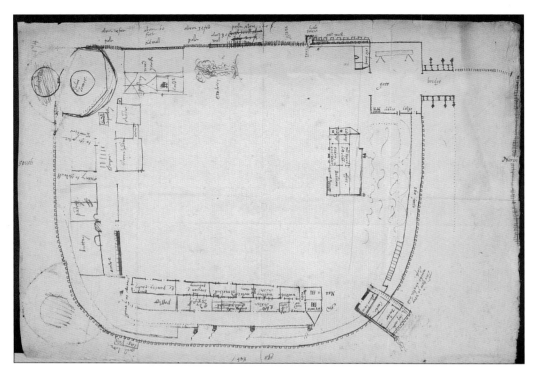

exercise by riding outside, she was escorted by a hundred horsemen. Because castles needed to be cleaned regularly, hers would be a dreary, peripatetic existence, moving from one damp, gloomy set of quarters to the next – Carlisle, Bolton, Tutbury, Wingfield Manor, Chatsworth, Chartley – the numbers in her household increasing and decreasing, as plots to free her came and went, and security levels rose and fell.

Previously an energetic, athletic young woman at the centre of affairs of state, Mary now had to occupy the empty hours in other ways. Her keeper for the longest period was George, 6th Earl of Shrewsbury, and Mary and his wife, the famous Bess of Hardwick, collaborated in sewing designs copied from woodcuts in emblem books. Intended to decorate bed curtains or wall-hangings, an impressive set is preserved in the care of the Victoria and Albert Museum. The panels completed by Mary herself have the letters 'MA' superimposed on the Greek letter *phi* (Φ), representing her first husband's initial 'F'. She had always loved reading, and when Mary travelled from one place to the next, a cartload of books went with her.

Pining for her small son, she imagined him growing into a faithful, loving boy who would somehow help her to regain her freedom.

Used to crowds of people around her, Mary sought solace in keeping small pets – little dogs and singing birds sent from France. Most importantly, she wrote long and impassioned letters to Elizabeth and to all her remaining friends on the Continent, protesting her innocence and begging for their assistance. From time to time she was allowed visitors, and when she began to suffer badly from arthritis she was permitted to visit Buxton to bathe in the medicinal waters. We know all too little about these occasions, but we do know that she met London courtiers at this fashionable spa, including Sir William Cecil himself, and her one time suitor, Robert, Earl of Leicester.

Mary had made it clear from the start that she regarded herself as being perfectly justified in seeking any possible means of escape, and eventually her involvement in plotting brought an end to her captivity, and to her life, when she became implicated in the conspiracy devised by Sir Anthony Babington.

Babington tried to instigate a foreign invasion which would result in Mary's release and the assassination of Queen Elizabeth, whom Mary would then replace on the throne of England. Sir Francis Walsingham, the

OPPOSITE, ABOVE

Plan of
Tutbury Castle.

*By John Somers,
31 December 1584*

CATALOGUE NO. 170

OPPOSITE, BELOW

The Marian Hanging,
embroidered by Mary,
Queen of Scots and others,
during her captivity.

1570–85

CATALOGUE NO. 178

BELOW

*Sir Francis Walsingham
(c.1532–90).*

*Attributed to John de
Critz the Elder, c.1587*

CATALOGUE NO. 189

BELOW, LEFT

*The Trial of Mary,
Queen of Scots.*

15 October 1586

CATALOGUE NO. 192

RIGHT

A copy of the Death
Warrant of Mary,
Queen of Scots.

1 February 1587

CATALOGUE NO. 193

English spy-master, had his men intercept the plotters' correspondence.

A coded letter from Mary, approving the plan, fell into his hands,
and for good measure he ordered one of his men to forge a postscript
from her, asking for the names of those who were to assassinate Queen
Elizabeth. Mary's fate was sealed.

On 11 August 1586, her unsympathetic keeper, Sir Amyas Paulet,
unexpectedly invited Mary to go hunting with him. As they rode out,
they were intercepted by a group of horsemen, whose leader charged
her with committing treason against Elizabeth I. Mary's belongings
were searched, her valuables confiscated, and on 21 September she was
moved to Fotheringhay Castle, Northamptonshire, which she knew
was used as a state prison. There, on 15 October, she was tried for
treason, protesting that no court had any jurisdiction over her, for she
was a monarch in her own right.

The Great Hall was filled with English peers, privy councillors and
officials that day. A throne had been set up at one end of the Hall, and
Mary exclaimed that she should be seated there. She was told that it was
Queen Elizabeth's throne, and it would remain empty. Allowed no law-
yers or defence witnesses and no access to her papers, she spent two days

asserting her innocence of planning Elizabeth's death. The courtiers then rode back to London and on 25 October they announced their verdict. She was guilty, and she would be executed.

Elizabeth, loathe to authorise the death of a sister Queen, procrastinated, but on 1 February 1587 she signed the fateful warrant, which has since vanished. Six days later, Mary was told that she was to die the following morning. She spent that night composing her will, making arrangements for the distribution of her few remaining belongings, and writing letters. The last one was to Henri III of France, her former brother-in-law. She rose at six o'clock the next morning, prayed in her oratory for more than an hour, and between eight and nine o'clock walked in procession to the Great Hall, her black dress concealing a red petticoat: red, the colour of the Resurrection. Trotting along beneath her skirts was one of her little pet dogs.

Reluctantly, the Earl of Kent allowed six of her servants to accompany her into the Hall. She mounted the scaffold and knelt, praying loudly in both Latin and in English. As was customary, the executioner asked her pardon for what he was about to do, and she replied that she forgave him with all her heart, for he would put an end to her troubles. When he and his assistant stepped forward to help her women take off her dress and veil, she smiled wryly, commenting with characteristic

MARY, QUEEN
OF SCOTS

59

BELOW

The Execution of Mary, Queen of Scots, in watercolour.

In watercolour, artist unknown, early 17th century

CATALOGUE NO. 197

*The Execution of Mary,
Queen of Scots*, an ink
and pencil sketch.

*Ink and pencil sketch,
artist unknown,
8 February 1587*

CATALOGUE NO. 196

gentle irony that never before had she employed such grooms of the
chamber. One of her women tied a gold-embroidered cloth round her
eyes. The Queen knelt and placed her neck on the block, saying loudly,
'Into your hands, O Lord, do I commend my soul'. With three strokes
of the axe, she was dead.

Afterwards, the block and her clothes were burned so that they could
not be kept as relics. Her little dog, rescued from the scene, refused to
eat, and died.

Sixteen years later, in 1603, Mary's son James VI united the crowns
of Scotland and England when he inherited the throne of Queen
Elizabeth I.

ABOVE

James VI and I, painted the year after
he inherited the throne of England.

By John de Critz the Elder, 1604

CATALOGUE NO. 210

EXHIBITION CATALOGUE

IN MY END IS MY BEGINNING

I. *THE BLAIRS MEMORIAL PORTRAIT OF MARY, QUEEN OF SCOTS*

Artist unknown, Flemish, early 17th century
Oil on canvas, 255 x 168 cm
Lent by Blairs Museum

This painting is one of the most familiar images of Mary. It was deliberately painted as a piece of political and religious propaganda to promote Mary's death as a Catholic martyr. The painting was commissioned by Elizabeth Curle, one of Mary's chamber-women, who, along with Jane Kennedy, attended Mary at her execution. According to Elizabeth Curle's will, she received a miniature portrait of Mary which may have been used as Mary's likeness for this painting. In 1620 Curle bequeathed the painting to the Scots College at Douai; and it was later sent to the Scots College in Paris, before, in 1833, reaching Blairs College, Aberdeen, a junior seminary for boys studying for the Catholic priesthood.

MARY'S ROYAL LIFELINE

2. ROYAL ARMS OF JAMES V

Maker unknown, possibly Scottish, *c.*1540
Oak panel, 75 x 55 cm
National Museums Scotland, acc. no. H.KL 202

This wooden panel was part of the decoration of the chapel of the Franciscan Nunnery in Dundee's Overgate, one of the burgh's oldest streets.

NB: Measurements are denoted in centimetres, and by height, width, then depth (unless otherwise indicated). The abbreviation 'acc. no.' stands for 'accession number'.

2.

3. WEDDING PORTRAIT OF JAMES V AND MARY OF GUISE

Artist unknown, possibly Scottish, *c.*1538
Oil on panel, 72.9 x 93.9 x 3 cm
From the Collection at Blair Castle, Perthshire

The couple were married in France on 9 May 1538. Mary was James's second wife. They had two sons, both of whom died in infancy. Mary, Queen of Scots was their only surviving child.

4. BOOK OF ACCOUNTS

Scottish, July 1548
Book, 33 x 48 cm (open)
Lent by National Records of Scotland

This Treasurer's Account records payment of 22 shillings to a royal messenger despatched to the port towns of Fife to recruit sailors for the galleys to take Mary to France.

5. *FRANÇOIS OF LORRAINE, DUKE OF GUISE*

By Léonard Limosin, French, 1557
Enamel on copper, 46.4 x 31.2 cm
Paris, musée du Louvre, département des Objets d'art

Mary's uncle François (1519–63) was head of the powerful Guise family. He was very close to Mary's father-in-law, King Henri II of France. As Henri's senior military commander, he successfully captured Calais from the English in 1558. Later that year, he helped to organise the wedding of Mary and the Dauphin François.

6. *CHARLES, CARDINAL OF LORRAINE*

By Léonard Limosin, French, c.1557
Enamel on copper, gilt wood frame, 73.8 x 57.8 cm
Lent by the Victoria and Albert Museum

Charles (1524–74) was the younger of the two principal Guise brothers. Also close to the monarch, he officiated at the coronation of three French kings, including Mary's husband, François II. Charles was involved with Mary's education and, on behalf of his older sister Mary of Guise, he jealously guarded his niece's status at the French court.

7. *CARDINAL DAVID BEATON*

Artist unknown, Scottish, early 16th century
Oil on canvas, 84.5 x 73 x 5 cm
Lent by Blairs Museum

Beaton (c.1494–1546) was Scotland's most senior Catholic cleric and the last pre-Reformation Scottish Cardinal. He was James V's ambassador to France, and was involved in both sets of French marriage negotiations on the King's behalf. He officiated at both the baptism and coronation of Mary, Queen of Scots.

8. EARLIEST KNOWN LETTER OF MARY, QUEEN OF SCOTS

French, c.1550
Paper, 21 x 31.5 cm
Lent by National Records of Scotland

Mary arrived in France in August 1548. In 1550 she wrote this letter in French to her mother, Mary of Guise, who had remained in Scotland. Mary writes that her French envoy, de Brézé, has 'instructions from the King to tell you all the latest news, which prevents me from writing you a longer letter'.

9. LETTER FROM THE DAUPHIN FRANÇOIS TO MARY OF GUISE

French, 1558
Paper, 30.5 x 20.3 cm
Lent by National Records of Scotland

9.

In this poignant letter the 14-year-old Dauphin François writes to Mary's mother, Mary of Guise, to tell her of his great happiness at the prospect of marrying her daughter.

10. MAP OF LEITH

English, 7 May 1560
Paper, 72.4 x 86.4 cm
On loan courtesy of Lord Egremont

This spy map shows the position of the English and Scottish forces as they made the final assault against the French troops who were garrisoned in the then fortified town of Leith.

11. *MARY, QUEEN OF SCOTS*, IN WHITE MOURNING

By François Clouet, c.1560–61
Oil on panel, 30.3 x 23.2 cm
Lent by the Royal Collection Trust on behalf of Her Majesty the Queen

Mary is wearing white, *en deuil blanc,* the traditional mourning colour of the French royal family. Within a period of 18 months, she had lost three close family members: her father-in-law Henri II of France died in July 1559 as a result of a jousting accident; her mother, Mary of Guise, died in June 1560; and in December 1560, she lost her young husband François II. Mary returned from France to her native Scotland in August 1561 and it is probable that this painting was made sometime between July 1559 and that date.

AULD AND NEW ALLIANCES

12. ATLAS

By Abraham Ortelius, Flanders, 1579
Book, 43 x 56.5 x 7 cm (open)
National Museums Scotland, acc. no. T.1908.64

This is a third edition of *Theatrum Orbis Terrarum*, or *Theatre of the World*, the first modern atlas, drawn by Abraham Ortelius, who was a pioneer Flemish cartographer. The Low Countries dominated chart production in the 16th century.

This map shows the political structure of Europe at the height of the Renaissance. In this period Continental Europe was dominated by a few large dynastic empires: France, Spain and the Holy Roman Empire, the latter centred on German-speaking Central Europe. Although Scotland and England were smaller independent kingdoms, they played their own part in the alliance system between the larger powers.

13. CARVED MEDALLION HEAD

Scottish, *c*.1540
Oak, 73 cm (diameter), 11 cm (depth)
National Museums Scotland, acc. no. H.KL 20

One of the 'Stirling Heads' from the ceiling of the Royal Palace at Stirling Castle – possibly the King's Inner Hall – representing Margaret Tudor (see page 66), sister of Henry VIII of England and mother of James V. She is holding a small greyhound, a breed of dog often used as a symbol for the House of Tudor.

14. CARVED MEDALLION HEAD

Scottish, *c*.1540
Oak, 73 cm (diameter), 11 cm (depth)
National Museums Scotland, acc. no. H.KL 19

Another 'Stirling Head', showing King James V. It is one of a number of the heads which represent both Scottish and foreign monarchs as a means of denoting James's dynastic position and his place in Renaissance Europe's monarchical alliance system.

13.

15.

IACOBVS · 4 · D · GRATIA
REX · SCOTVRIA

THE ROYAL HOUSE OF STEWART

15. *JAMES IV (1473–1513, reigned 1488–1513)*

Artist unknown, possibly Scottish, early 16th century
Oil on panel, 41.2 x 33 cm
Lent by the Scottish National Portrait Gallery, Edinburgh

James IV succeeded his father James III, who was killed after the Battle of Sauchieburn. James IV also died a violent death, killed on the battlefield, fighting against the English at Flodden. As part of an earlier desire to make peace with England, James had married Margaret Tudor, the daughter of Henry VII, in 1503.

16. THE LINDSAY ARMORIAL

By Sir David Lindsay, Scottish, 1542
Book, 29 x 40 cm (open)
Lent by the National Library of Scotland

This Scottish Heraldic Armorial was compiled by the Lord Lyon King of Arms, Sir David Lindsay of the Mount (1466–1555) in 1542. This is Scotland's earliest existing Register of Arms and it is noted for its comprehensive and beautiful depiction of the arms of Scotland and its nobility. It provided the model for other armorial collections, including the Forman Armorial below.

17. THE FORMAN ARMORIAL

By Sir Robert Forman, Scottish, *c.*1562
Book, 40.5 x 27.9 cm
Lent by the National Library of Scotland

Forman of Luthrie succeeded Sir David Lindsay as Lord Lyon in 1555, a position which he held until his death in 1567. This Armorial was compiled around 1562 for presentation to Mary, Queen of Scots and is noted for its delightful representations of Scotland's past kings and queens. Forman is known to have compiled at least three such collections of arms.

17.

THE ARMES OF ALLIACE BETVIX
THE DOLPHIN OF FRANCE AND
MARIE QVENE OF SCOTLAND

18. UNICORN, OF JAMES V

Minted in Edinburgh, 1513–26
Gold, 2.7 cm (diameter)
National Museums Scotland,
acc. no. H.C147

King James V's coin designs
reflect his ambitions to be seen as
a Renaissance monarch.

19. GROAT, OF JAMES V

Minted in Edinburgh, 1526–39
Silver, 2.6 cm (diameter)
National Museums Scotland,
acc. no. H.C19110

20. DUCAT, OF JAMES V

Minted in Edinburgh, 1539
Gold, 2.4 cm (diameter)
National Museums Scotland,
acc. no. H.C162

21. TWO-THIRDS DUCAT, OF JAMES V

Minted in Edinburgh, 1540
Gold, 2 cm (diameter)
National Museums Scotland,
acc. no. H.C163

22. FLOOR TILE FROM LINLITHGOW PALACE

Probably Scottish, early 16th
century
Glazed earthenware,
20.8 x 20.5 x 3.5 cm
Lent by Historic Scotland

Linlithgow Palace was remodelled by James IV as a wedding
gift to Margaret Tudor, daughter
of Henry VII of England. The
central stamp of this tile bears
the monogram of James IV and
his wife Margaret Tudor inter-
twined with a love-knot.

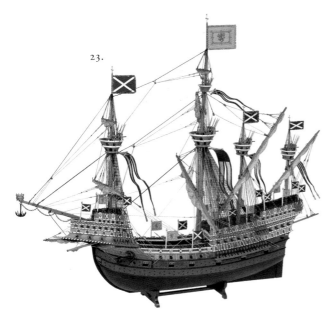
23.

23. SHIP MODEL

Scottish, 20th century
110 cm (height), 122.5 cm (width, bowsprit to stern),
40 cm (depth)
National Museums Scotland, acc. no. M.1932.66
Image is of ship donated by R. Patterson (acc. no.
T.1926.20), another version of the *Michael*

Completed in 1511, the great *Michael* was the flagship of the Royal Scots Navy. The *Michael* was
enormous, as much as 73 metres long, and weighed
1000 tons. This warship required a crew of over 300
sailors, and the wages bill for the crew amounted to
ten per cent of the Crown's income.

24. 'DESCRITTIONE DEL L'ISOLA DI SCOTIA'

By Tommaso Porcacchi, Venice, 1572
Map, 43 x 57 cm
National Museums Scotland, acc. no. T.2003.309.170

This is one of the earliest printed maps of Scotland,
from Tommaso Poracchi's work *L'Isola Pui Famosa
del Mondo* (*The Most Famous Islands in the World*).

HOUSE OF TUDOR

25. LECTERN

Low Countries or Scotland, early 16th century
Brass, 168 cm (height), 55 cm (diameter of base)
Lent by St Stephen's Church, St Albans, by permission
of the Vicar, Churchwardens and the Parochial Church
Council

This lectern was taken from the Abbey Church of
Holyrood by the English soldier, Sir Richard Lee of
Sopwell, in 1544 as spoils of war during the Rough
Wooing. Known as the 'Dunkeld Lectern', it was
probably presented to Holyrood Abbey by George
Crichton when he was appointed Bishop of Dunkeld
in the 1520s. He had been Abbot at Holyrood Abbey
from about 1515 to 1524.

26. CHEST

Maker unknown, Scottish, early 16th century
Oak, 50 x 92 x 42 cm
On loan from a Private Collection

This chest is associated with James IV and his wife,
Margaret Tudor. The front left-hand panel has the
love-knot with the monogram 'I&M', representing
James and Margaret who married on 8 August 1503.
James is represented by the letter 'I' as there was no
'J' in the alphabet at this time. Conjoined initials
are linked to marriage and the giving of wedding
gifts.

27. SOVEREIGN, OF HENRY VIII

Minted in London, 1509–44
Gold, 4.2 cm (diameter of both)
National Museums Scotland, acc. nos A.1911.506.124
(obverse) and A.1911.506.125 (reverse)

Coins were an important means of emphasising the
dynastic aspirations of a sovereign.

28. CROWN, OF EDWARD VI

Minted in London, 1551–53
Silver, 4.1 cm (diameter)
National Museums Scotland, acc. nos A.1915.65
(obverse) and A.1915.67 (reverse)

29. SOVEREIGN, OF ELIZABETH I

Minted in London, 1584–89
Gold, 4.4 cm (diameter)
National Museums Scotland, acc. no. A.1911.506.166

30. RYAL, OF ELIZABETH I

Minted in London, 1584–89
Gold, c.3.65 cm (diameter)
National Museums Scotland, acc. no. A.1911.506.174

31.

31. SHIP MODEL

By R. Patterson, Scottish, 20th century
Wood, 93 cm (height), 42 cm (width), 108 cm (length),
made to a scale of 1:48
National Museums Scotland, acc. no. T.1959.22

This is a model of the *Mary Willoughby*. The original
was built as an armed merchantman for the English
Royal Navy. The ship was captured by the Scots in
1536 and used as the flagship of the Scottish Royal
Navy. It was recaptured by the English during the
wars of the Rough Wooing in 1547.

32. MODEL OF HENRY VIII

By Victoria Cairns, Scottish, 21st century
Lent by The Lady of Finavon

As very little historical costume from this period
survives, costume historians draw many of their
references from paintings, sculptures, books and
manuscripts. This model has been largely created
from the portrait by an unknown artist based on the
Whitehall Mural painted by Hans Holbein in 1537.

VALOIS AND GUISE

33. THE FINGASK CHALICE

Made in Paris or the surrounding area, c.1509–10
Silver gilt and basse-taille enamel, 18 cm (height),
13.3 cm (diameter)
National Museums Scotland, acc. no. A.1993.70

The foot is engraved with Saint Denis, an early
bishop of Paris, who was martyred around AD 250.
Most French kings were buried in the Abbey of
Saint Denis, near Paris.

33.

34.

35.

34. MIRROR BACK

By the Master 'I. D. C.', Limoges, c.1580–1600
Enamel and foil on copper, 11.3 cm (length), 8.6 cm
(width)
National Museums Scotland, acc. no. A.1868.35.2

The upper half is decorated with the classical god-
dess Diana, who is hunting. The woman in Hell may
be Prosperine, who was abducted by Pluto, the ruler
of the Underworld. It may also be a reference to
Diane de Poitiers, the mistress of King Henri II.

35. PART OF A POLEYN OR KNEE ARMOUR

French, c.1550–60
Steel, 13 x 11.6 cm (maximum width)
National Museums Scotland, acc. no. A.1969.143

Embossed with a mask of tragedy, this is related to
parts of armour that were probably made for King
Henri II of France.

36. PORTRAIT TESTON, OF HENRI II

Minted in Montpellier, France, 1557
Silver, 2.9 cm (diameter)
National Museums Scotland, acc. no. A.1931.160

37. PORTRAIT TESTON, OF FRANÇOIS I

Minted in Lyon, France, 1515–40
Silver, 2.9 cm (diameter)
National Museums Scotland, acc. no. A.1931.176

38. TESTOON, OF MARY AND FRANÇOIS

Minted in Edinburgh, 1558–60
Silver, 2.95 cm (diameter of both)
National Museums Scotland, acc. nos H.C4028
(obverse) and H.C4029 (reverse)

This coin was worth five shillings Scots.

39. PORTRAIT TESTOON, OF MARY, QUEEN OF SCOTS

Minted in Edinburgh, 1561–62
Silver, 2.9 cm (diameter)
National Museums Scotland, acc. no. H.C4082

The profile of Mary is thought to be after a portrait
by François Clouet. It shows Mary in the early years
of her first widowhood.

40. *DAUPHIN FRANÇOIS*

By Léonard Limosin, French, c.1553
Enamel on copper, gold highlights, 44.8 x 31.9 cm
Paris, musée du Louvre, département des Objets d'art

Enamelled portraits were particularly fashionable at
this time and those by Limosin were especially valued
for their artistic merit and technical skill. Although
he was only nine years old, the Dauphin's status is
indicated by the pendant insignia of the Order of
Saint Michel.

41. *MARY, QUEEN OF SCOTS*

By François Clouet, 1558
Watercolour on vellum, 30 x 18 cm
Lent by the Royal Collection Trust on behalf of Her
Majesty the Queen

Mary is depicted placing a ring on the fourth finger
of the right hand, a symbolic gesture thought to
allude to her marriage to the Dauphin François.

42. HAND BELL

Maker unknown, 16th century
Silver gilt, 9.4 cm (height), 5.6 cm (diameter)
On loan from a Private Collection

This hand bell is engraved with the Royal Arms
of Scotland and the monogram of Mary and the
Dauphin François. A 'little silver bell' is mentioned
in an inventory of Mary's jewels drawn up by
Elizabeth Curle, one of Mary's chamber-women,
after the execution.

43. FESTIVAL BOOK. PUBLISHED IN PARIS FOR THE MARRIAGE OF MARY, QUEEN OF SCOTS AND THE DAUPHIN FRANÇOIS

Paris, c.1558
Book, 17 x 22.6 cm (open)
Lent by The British Library

44.
(OBVERSE)

(REVERSE)

Festival books were published as official illustrated
accounts of state festivities and royal events such as
entries to a city. They presented an idealised version
of events rather than a strict factual account.

44. DUCAT, OF MARY, QUEEN OF SCOTS AND FRANÇOIS, DAUPHIN OF FRANCE

Minted in Edinburgh, 1558
Gold, 3.1 mm (diameter)
National Museums Scotland, acc. no. H.C183

This ducat was produced to celebrate the royal
wedding.

45. *COAT OF ARMS OF MARY, QUEEN OF SCOTS*

French, c.1559
Ink drawing on paper, 31.5 x 19.5 cm
Paris, Bibliothèque nationale de France, départment des
Manuscrits

These arms were very controversial as they included
the arms of England. This implied that Mary had
claims to Elizabeth I's throne, which caused uproar
in England.

46. CUP OR TAZZA

By Jean de Court (called Vigier), 1556
Enamelled copper, grisaille, 17 x 13.5 cm
Paris, Bibliothèque nationale de France, départment des Monnais, médailles et antiques

This cup, decorated with the arms of Scotland, was made by one of the most accomplished enamel painters of the Limoges school. It is a very rare piece and has been painted in grisaille, a term used to describe a form of painting in shades of grey.

RENAISSANCE

47. PENDANT IN THE FORM OF AN ELEPHANT ON A PLATFORM

Probably Italian, 16th century
Gold, enamel, rubies, emeralds and pearls, 7 cm (length), 4 cm (width), 2.5 cm (depth)
National Museums Scotland, acc. no. A.1960.385

48. PENDANT IN THE FORM OF A POODLE

German, 16th century
Gold, enamel, rubies and pearls, 6 cm (length), 2.4 cm (width), 0.6 cm (depth)
National Museums Scotland, acc. no. A.1917.59

Replacing the mediaeval brooch, the pendant was the most important piece of jewellery in the Renaissance period. Frequently designed to be viewed from both sides, their backs were often elaborately enamelled.

49. GOBLET

By Jacopo Verzelini and engraved by Anthony de Lysle at Crutched Friars Glasshouse, English, c.1590
Glass with diamond-point engraving, 18.6 cm (height), 8 cm (diameter of foot)
National Museums Scotland, acc. no. A.1967.400

In 1574 Elizabeth I granted Verzelini exclusive rights for 21 years to produce 'Venetian' glass in England. Imports from Italy were forbidden, a ban that lasted until 1623 and made Verzelini unpopular with London's merchants.

47.

48.

50. *ASTRONOMIQUE DISCOURS*

By James Bassantin, Lyon, France, 1557
Book, 43.5 x 61 cm (open)
Lent by the National Library of Scotland

James Bassantin (before 1513 to 1568) was a Scottish astronomer and mathematician who spent a large part of his life in France. Bassantin was said to have made two uncanny predictions: first, 'that there would be at length captivity and utter wreck for Mary, Queen of Scots, at the hands of Elizabeth I'; and second, that 'England would at length fall of right to the crown of Scotland'. He was an example of a Scottish Renaissance scholar who maintained close links with Europe.

51. THE CADBOLL CUP

Maker unknown, Scottish, late 16th century
Silver, parcel-gilt, 15.3 cm (height), 10.7 cm (diameter of base), 16.3 cm (diameter of rim)
National Museums Scotland, acc. no. H.MEQ 958

This important cup represents a contemporary fusion of Scottish West Highland decoration in the bowl's panels with French Renaissance strap work on the stem. Scottish craftsmen were inspired by the new ideas from the Continent, particularly France, given the strong cultural links between the two countries.

52. POCKET COMPENDIUM DIAL

By Humphrey Cole, English, 1575
Gilt-brass, with sundial, compass and calendar combined, 5.5 x 12 x 5.2 cm
National Museums Scotland, acc. no. H.NL 18

Combining the functions of a sundial, compass and calendar, such dials were sought after by those interested in the scientific advances of the Renaissance. Cole was the first native-born English scientific instrument-maker and supplied navigation instruments to the explorer Martin Frobisher, although his main employment was at the Mint.

53. ASTROLABE

Probably by Jean Fusoris (c.1365–1436), French, early 15th century
Brass, 15 cm (height), 13 cm (diameter), 2 cm (depth)
National Museums Scotland, acc. no. T.1947.27

An astrolabe is a many-purposed instrument, used by navigators, astronomers and astrologers for locating and predicting the positions of the Sun, Moon, planets and stars at particular latitudes; determining local time; surveying; triangulation; and casting horoscopes. This working example was later owned by Robert Gordon of Straloch (1580–1661), who had additions made for Edinburgh and Aberdeen. He was one of Scotland's most talented early map-makers and mathematicians.

51.

52.

54. PLATE FROM AN ACCOUCHEMENT SET

Italian, 1575–1600
Maiolica (tin-glazed earthenware) painted in poly-
chrome, 20.4 cm (diameter)
National Museums Scotland, acc. no. A.231.2

Accouchement sets were made as a gift for women
during confinement. A set usually consisted of a
broth bowl on a raised foot (its cover in the form of
a plate), a bowl or cup, and a salt-cellar and its
domed pierced cover.

55. JUG

By Patanazzi workshop, Italian, c.1579
Maiolica (tin-glazed earthenware) painted in poly-
chrome, 26.5 cm (height) x 14.5 cm (diameter)
National Museums Scotland, acc. no. A.1885.32

From a service made to celebrate the marriage of
Alfonso II d'Este, Duke of Ferrara, and Margarita
Gonzaga in 1579.

55.

56. EWER

By Niccolo Sisti workshop or Montelupo, Italian, 1590s
Maiolica (tin-glazed earthenware) painted in poly-
chrome, 16 x 11 x 9.3 cm
National Museums Scotland, acc. no. K.2003.1055

This ewer is from the wreck of a merchant vessel,
probably from the Iberian Peninsula, discovered at
Kinlochbervie, Sutherland, in 1997. The presence of
a Mediterranean merchant ship at the northernmost
tip of Scotland is probably related to developing
Iberian trade using a route around Scotland to avoid
the English Channel during the political uncertain-
ties at the end of the 16th century.

57. TABLE CLOCK

By Bartholomew Newsum, English, late 16th century
Brass, 17 cm (height), 13 cm (diameter)
National Museums Scotland, acc. no. T.1978.112

This is one of only three surviving clocks made
by Bartholomew Newsum, Clockmaker to Queen
Elizabeth I and one of the first British clockmakers.
The coats of arms on the clock indicate that it was
probably made for Margaret Stanley, Countess of
Derby. For a time she was potentially heir to Queen
Elizabeth I, but she died before the Queen. Elaborately decorated clocks such as this represented the
amalgamation of art and science fashionable during
the Renaissance, and were the height of luxury,
displaying the prestige of their owners.

57.

59.

60.

58. PHILIP II'S *GREAT ASTROLABE*

English, 1876
Electrotype of bronze original from 1566,
37 cm (height), 60 cm (diameter), 6.5 cm (depth)
National Museums Scotland, acc. no. T.1931.270

The original of this splendid display piece was made by the greatest instrument-maker of the day, Walter Arsenius of Louvain in Flanders, in 1566, for King Philip II of Spain. The Low Countries were part of the Holy Roman Empire, as was Spain, and the development of scientific instruments helped explorers to find their way to the New World and back, using astrolabes and other navigation devices.

59. BEAKER

Late Chimú, South American, *c.*15th century
Gold, 12.2 cm (height), 5.9 cm (diameter of base),
10.5 cm (diameter of rim)
National Museums Scotland, acc. no. A.1947.170

The Chimú were a people who had settled on the coastline of present-day Peru, and were noted for their fine metal-working. Only a handful of such gold beakers escaped the melting-pot of the 16th-century Spanish conquerors. Spain was one of the first European powers to expand into the New World.

60. TAPESTRY FRAGMENT

Flemish, 16th century
Coloured wool, silk, 238.8 x 162.6 cm
National Museums Scotland, acc. no. A.1956.1439

This tapestry fragment shows a European bison and a Dragon's Blood tree. By the 16th century the European bison was restricted to Poland. The rare Dragon's Blood was native to the Canary Islands, and other Spanish and Portuguese Atlantic islands. The Renaissance was an age in which Europe's knowledge of the wider world was expanding.

61. *JOHN KNOX (C.1514–72), REFORMER AND HISTORIAN*

Artist unknown, after Adrian Vanson, 1580
Wood engraving on paper, 15.2 x 11.4 cm
Lent by the Scottish National Portrait Gallery, Edinburgh
Bequeathed by W. F. Watson in 1886

This woodcut was based on a posthumous portrait of the famous Reformer, painted in Edinburgh seven years after his death, by an artist who probably knew him, or had at least seen him. It was used as a book illustration and subsequently became the inspiration for many history pictures and statues.

62. *FIRST BLAST OF THE TRUMPET AGAINST THE MONSTROUS REGIMENT OF WOMEN*

By John Knox, Swiss, 1558
Tract, 14 x 19 cm
Lent by the National Library of Scotland

This tract was aimed against Europe's Catholic women rulers, especially Mary Tudor and Mary of Guise. Knox claimed that the Bible opposed the rule of women over men.

63. NEW TESTAMENT AND PSALTER

English, 1619 and 1621
Silver, silver-gilt thread work, paper, 11 x 8.5 x 4 cm
National Museums Scotland, acc. no. H.RHF 1

The ability of ordinary people to read the Bible was central to the theology of the Reformation. The Psalms were a form of hymn derived from the Psalms of David, one of the books of the Old Testament.

64. *THE FORM OF PRAYERS AND MINISTRATION OF THE SACRAMENTS*

Geneva, 1565
Book, 13.5 x 19 cm (open)
Lent by the National Library of Scotland

This Reformed order of service was used by the English congregation at Geneva. It was based on an earlier version written by John Knox while minister of the English congregation at Frankfurt. After the Scottish Reformation it was adopted by the new Protestant Kirk.

65. *THE FIRST BOOK OF DISCIPLINE*

Amsterdam, 1621
Book, 19 x 25 cm (open)
Lent by the National Library of Scotland

In 1560 John Knox and five other ministers compiled this treatise outlining the structure, practice and governance of the new reformed Protestant Kirk. It was first printed in 1621. It proposed a school for every parish in Scotland to teach basic literacy to allow Scots to read the Bible for themselves, but lack of funding made this impossible for many years.

66. COMMUNION CUP

By John Mosman, Edinburgh, 1585–86
Silver, 9.5 cm (diameter of base), 23 cm (diameter of rim)
National Museums Scotland, acc. no. H.KJ 253

This Communion cup, the earliest surviving cup made purposely for Reformed Church use, belonged to Roseneath Kirk, Dunbartonshire. It has the same form as a domestic wine cup. Some Catholic clerics denounced Protestants for using everyday 'basins and tavern cups' for dispensing Holy Communion.

67. THE MARY CUP

By Christopher Lindenberger, German, *c.*1550–1600
Silver gilt, 41 cm (height) x 14.1 cm (diameter)
Lent by Perth Museum & Art Gallery

Although this cup has become associated with Mary, Queen of Scots, it is more likely to have belonged to a wealthy parishioner who gave it to the Kirk about 1630 for use at Communion. The irony of the cup's alleged connection to the Catholic Mary is that St John's Kirk was the scene of one of Knox's sermons which launched the Reformation in Scotland.

68. BOOK OF HOURS OF MARY OF GUISE

French, late 15th century
13.5 x 20 cm (open)
Lent by the National Library of Scotland

This illuminated manuscript Book of Hours belonged to Mary of Guise, the mother of Mary, Queen of Scots. It is signed 'Marie R'.

69. CRUCIFIX

Scottish, 15th or 16th century
Silver, ebony, 7.4 x 5.8 x 1.3 cm
National Museums Scotland, acc. no. H.KE 16

This is known as the Craigmillar Crucifix as it was found in 'Queen Mary's Room' at Craigmillar Castle, Edinburgh. Discovered before 1815, it has become associated with Mary.

70. THE FETTERNEAR BANNER

Scottish, made *c.*1520
Linen with silk embroidery, 180 x 96 cm
National Museums Scotland, acc. no. H.LF 23

This is the only known church banner to survive
from medieval Scotland. It was intended to be
carried in church processions and was probably
made for the Confraternity of the Holy Blood, a
religious group who worshipped in St Giles' Kirk,
Edinburgh.

71. LOCKET

Maker unknown, 16th century
Gold and enamels, 4.1 x 2.3 x 0.8 cm
On loan from a Private Collection

According to a family tradition, this locket, known
as the 'Mary, Queen of Scots Jewel', was presented
to Thomas Andrews, Sheriff of Northampton, by
Mary just before her execution. Accounts of the
execution do record Andrews' presence at the event
and Mary's distribution of jewels to her household
immediately prior to her death.

72. CHASUBLE

Scottish, late 15th or early 16th century
Gilt thread, silk, gilt braid, velvet, 109 x 70 cm
Lent by Blairs Museum

The chasuble is the outermost vestment worn by
a priest while celebrating Mass. On the central
embroidered panel are depictions of a pelican for
piety and St Andrew to the right of the Crucifixion
scene. The colour red is significant as it honours the
martyrs of the Catholic faith.

71.

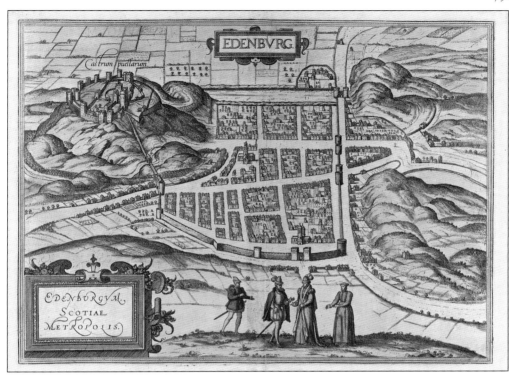

A CAPITAL CITY

73. MAP FROM *CIVITATES ORBIS TERRARUS*

By Georg Braun and Frans Hogenberg, German,
possibly 1582
Framed, mounted and in colour, 58.5 x 68 cm
National Museums Scotland, acc. no. T.2003.309.1

This plan, from an atlas of European cities, shows
Edinburgh from the south. The Flodden Wall surrounding the city was still prominent.

74. FIELD GUN AND CARRIAGE

Scottish: gun, early 16th century
Bronze, wood: gun 126.4 cm (length), 18 cm (maximum
width), 8 cm (maximum diameter); carriage 86.4 cm
(height), 52.1 cm (width), 86.4 (length)
National Museums Scotland, acc. no. H.LH 429

This small field gun, known as a falcon, was
probably made in the Scottish royal gun foundry in
Edinburgh Castle. The top of the gun is crudely
engraved with a cross potent, as featured on Mary,
Queen of Scots' coins issued by her mother, Mary
of Guise, as Regent.

75. CANNONBALL

Scottish, 16th century
Stone, 46–45 cm (diameter)
Lent by Historic Scotland

This cannonball from Edinburgh Castle is associated with Mons Meg. Mons Meg was fired during
the celebrations for the marriage of Mary and the
Dauphin François. A servant was sent two miles to
retrieve the cannonball.

76.

76. THE GALLOWAY MAZER

By James Gray, Scottish, 1569
Silver gilt, maplewood bowl, 20.7 cm (height), 14 cm
(diameter of foot), 22.2 cm (diameter of rim)
National Museums Scotland, acc. no. H.MEQ 148

This high-status drinking cup, known as a mazer,
was made for Archibald Stewart, who became the
Provost of Edinburgh in 1579. By the middle of the
16th century, Edinburgh and its neighbouring burghs
were flourishing. Some members of their trade
incorporations, especially the goldsmiths, became
wealthy and influential.

77. GOLD MEDAL

By Michael Gilbert II, Scottish, 1562
Gold, 3.2 cm (diameter)
National Museums Scotland, acc. no. H.1967.436

This medal was made for George, Lord Seton, and
his wife, Isabella Hamilton. Seton was Master of
Mary's Household and a life-long supporter of his
queen. He was one of the capital's leading citizens,
having served as Provost from 1557 until 1559. His
country home, Seton Palace in East Lothian, was a
popular retreat for Mary.

78. NECKLACE

Late 16th or early 17th century
Gold enamel, pearls, rubies, garnets, 26 cm (length),
17.5 cm (width), 1 cm (depth)
On loan from a Private Collection

This is part of a collar which belonged to the Seton
family and is said to have been given by Mary, Queen
of Scots to Mary Seton, one of the Four Maries.
Mary Seton served the Queen during her captivity
and only left her service in 1583, retiring to France
due to her failing health.

79. *MINIATURE OF JAMES DOUGLAS, 4TH EARL OF MORTON (c.1516–81)*

Scottish, 19th century
Oil on copper, 6.2 x 4.6 x 4 cm
National Museums Scotland, acc. no. H.NT 270

Morton is alleged to have introduced the design on
which the Maiden, a type of guillotine used in
Edinburgh, was based. Ironically he met his own
death on the Maiden when he was executed in 1581,
partly for his implication in the murder of Henry,
Lord Darnley.

79.

80.

81.

80. CARVED ARMORIAL PANEL

Scottish, mid-16th century
Oak, 77 x 76 x 13 cm
National Museums Scotland, acc. no. H.KL 61

This panel from Linlithgow Palace has two versions of the Royal Arms of Scotland. It is thought that the intention was to show the arms of Mary below those of her father, James V. The lower version has been deliberately defaced.

81. CARVED MEDALLION HEAD

Scottish, c.1540
Oak, 73 cm (diameter), 11 cm (depth)
National Museums Scotland, acc. no. H.KL 113

This 'Stirling Head', from a ceiling in the Royal Palace at Stirling Castle, depicts a *putto* – a dancing cherub. Stirling Palace was a spectacular example of Renaissance style, as introduced by James V.

82. DOOR

Scottish, mid-16th century
Oak, 172 x 140 x 9 cm
National Museums Scotland, acc. no. H.1993.80

This door has been carved in the Renaissance style with the arms of Gordon of Huntly. A major aim of Mary's royal progress of the summer of 1562 was the subjugation of the Earl of Huntly, one of north-east Scotland's most powerful noblemen.

83. FRAGMENTS FROM THE LINLITHGOW PALACE FOUNTAIN

Scottish, c.1538
Stone, 109 x 48 x 45 cm
Lent by Historic Scotland

James V remodelled parts of Linlithgow Palace and added an elaborate fountain in the courtyard. This fragment has finely-carved details, including a lion's head and foliage decoration. Linlithgow was used by the Stewart monarchs as a retreat from the formal court at Holyroodhouse and Stirling.

THE QUEEN'S MOTHER

84. *MARIE DE LORRAINE (MARY OF GUISE), QUEEN OF SCOTS*

Attributed to François Clouet, French, c.1550–51
Chalk on paper, 30.2 x 22.4 cm
Lent by The British Museum

Mary of Guise, mother of Mary, Queen of Scots, was born on 20 November 1515 in north-east France into the powerful Guise family, with close links to France's ruling Valois dynasty. First married to the Duke of Longueville, as a young widow she then became the wife of James V, King of Scots, on 9 May 1538. She was crowned Queen of Scots on 22 February 1540. This chalk drawing was done by the artist in 1550–51.

85. DOOR LATCH

Scottish, 16th century
Iron, 30.1 x 7.7 x 3.5 cm
National Museums Scotland, acc. no. A.1905.988

Mary of Guise used several residences when in Edinburgh. This iron latch with thistle and *fleur-de-lis* terminals comes from Mary of Guise's house in the Canongate, Edinburgh.

86. KEY

Scottish or English, 16th century
Steel, 8.3 x 3.3 x 0.7 cm
National Museums Scotland, acc. no. A.1910.133

The bow on this key is surmounted by a crown. The key is said to have come from Mary of Guise's supposed house in Blyth's Close, just off Castle Hill, Edinburgh.

85. 86.

87. DOOR

Scottish, mid-16th century
Oak, 182 x 87 x 8 cm
National Museums Scotland, acc. no. H.KL 38

This door is said to be from Mary of Guise's house, at Blyth's Close, just off Castle Hill. This was one of the properties at which Mary of Guise occasionally stayed while visiting Edinburgh during the regency of the Earl of Arran. Mary and Arran were political rivals for power, with Mary finally ousting Arran as Regent in 1554.

88. DECORATIVE CARVING

Scottish, 16th century
Oak, 126.2 x 20.5 x 4.5 cm and 125.5 x 20 x 4.5 cm
National Museums Scotland, acc. nos H.KL 147.1 and H.KL 147.2

These oak swags, said to be from Mary of Guise's house at Blyth's Close, Edinburgh, are carved with fruit, flowers and leaves.

89. *JAMES HAMILTON, EARL OF ARRAN, DUKE OF CHÂTELHERAULT, REGENT OF SCOTLAND 1543–54*

Attributed to Arnold Bronckorst, Scottish, 1578
Oil on panel, 115.6 x 108 cm
Lent by His Grace The Duke of Hamilton, Lennoxlove, Haddington

Hamilton (*c*.1516–75) was a great-grandson of James II, making him first in line to the Scottish throne after Mary. When James V died he became Regent for the infant Queen Mary, despite the best efforts of his bitter rival Cardinal Beaton. He held the regency until 1554, when he had to resign in favour of Mary of Guise. As head of the powerful Hamilton family, he always put their interests first. This partly explains the apparent fickleness of his allegiances.

90. *MARY, QUEEN OF SCOTS (1542–87)*

Artist unknown, possibly French, possibly early 17th
century
Oil on canvas, 180 x 148 cm
Lent by Blairs Museum

The costume in this portrait is in keeping with
French fashion of the 1560s. While there are
similarities to some of the other earlier paintings
of Mary, many depictions of her were made after
her death. There is some uncertainty about the
identity of the sitter. Some art historians believe
that the painting was probably commissioned by
one of Mary's later supporters 40 years after her
death.

91. CAMEO PENDANT

Scottish, late 16th century
Gold, enamels, chalcedony, diamonds and a native-cut
ruby, 9.5 x 5.6 x 1.5 cm
National Museums Scotland, acc. no. H.NF 33

The central cameo depicting Mary and the high-
quality enamelled back-plate are of French or Italian
work, and have been set into a surround probably
made by a Scottish goldsmith. Mary brought
numerous cameos with her from France as gifts for
friends and supporters.

92. NECKLACE OF POMANDER BEADS

Possibly French, 16th century
Gold filigree, 36 cm (length), 1.2 cm (maximum
diameter of bead)
National Museums Scotland, acc. no. H.NA 421

This necklace is part of the Penicuik Jewels, said
to have been given by Mary to Gilles Mowbray, an
ancestor of the Clerk of Penicuik family. The beads
originally would have held perfume and are properly
known as paternoster beads because they usually
formed a rosary. The necklace is thought to have
been made up from the pair of gold bracelets that
Mary gave Gilles immediately before her execution.

91. (FRONT)

91. (BACK)

92.

93. PENDANT LOCKET SET WITH MINIATURE PORTRAITS

Scottish, late 16th century
Gold, enamel and seed pearls, 7.1 x 4.2 x 0.8 cm
National Museums Scotland, acc. no. H.NA 422

Also part of the Penicuik Jewels, it is believed that the miniatures may represent Mary and her son, James VI. It is possible this type of jewel may have been commissioned by the Queen specifically to give to her friends and supporters as part of royal 'gift giving', rather than from her personal collection.

94. PENDANT LOCKET SET WITH MINIATURE PORTRAITS

Scottish, late 16th century
Gold, enamel and seed pearls, 5.6 x 3.4 x 0.5 cm
National Museums Scotland, acc. no. H.NF 74

This type of locket may be the 'frames for pictures' often mentioned in the accounts of the Edinburgh goldsmith, George Heriot.

95. PENDANT LOCKET SET WITH MINIATURE PORTRAITS

Scottish, late 16th century
Gold, enamel, 4.4 x 3.5 cm
National Museums Scotland, acc. no. H.NA 520

This damaged locket was excavated near Corswall Castle in Wigtonshire. These lockets are very similar in construction, and recent scientific analysis undertaken by the Museum indicates that they are all of gold of similar quality. Although probably not made by the same craftsman, they may have come from the same workshop.

96. SIR ALEXANDER FRASER OF PHILORTH AND HIS WIFE, ELIZABETH MAXWELL

Miniatures on vellum, late 16th to early 17th century
Gold and crystal, set as ear-rings in the 18th century,
1.4 x 0.9 x 0.4 cm
National Museums Scotland, acc. no. H.NI 21 A and B

These miniature pictures are originally from another of these 'frames for pictures' and represent a uniquely Scottish style of jewellery.

93. (FRONT)

(BACK)

97. FINGER RING SET WITH A CARVED CAMEO OF MARY, QUEEN OF SCOTS

Cameo, 16th century; ring setting, 19th century
Gold and chalcedony; cameo 2.1 x 1.5 x 0.4 cm;
ring 1.9 cm (diameter)
On loan from Mr and Mrs Geoffrey Munn

98. PENDANT, SET WITH ARMS OF MARY, QUEEN OF SCOTS

19th century
Gold, enamel and glass, 5.2 x 2.8 x 0.3 cm
National Museums Scotland, acc. no. H.NA 588

The arms shown here are taken from the heraldic
signet ring [cat. no. 105] and represent Mary's arms
for the period 1548–58. It is now thought that the
glass centre and enamelled frame are 19th-century
copies made as part of the Romantic revival of
interest in Mary.

99. MAN'S DOUBLET

Possibly Italian, c.1550–60
Satin, canvas, with silk buttons, 61 cm (maximum
height) x 58 cm (maximum width)
National Museums Scotland, acc. no. A.1983.791

This doublet is of padded red satin lined in canvas,
trimmed with small hand-made silk buttons, possibly for use under light armour.

100. INVENTORY OF BOOKS, ORNAMENTS AND MASQUING CLOTHES BELONGING TO MARY, QUEEN OF SCOTS

Scottish, 1569
Inventory, 34 x 23 cm
Lent by National Records of Scotland

This is an inventory of goods given by Servais de
Condé, Mary's *valet-de-chambre*, to John Wood and
James Murray, servitors of the Regent Moray in
November 1569. Mary was now a captive of Elizabeth
I and much of her estate had been sold or redistri-
buted. The colourful masquing costumes listed are
in direct contrast to the sombre black and white
apparel Mary is often portrayed wearing.

101. THE MORTON VALANCES

French and/or Scottish, c.1580–90
Linen, wool, silk, 56 x 177 cm
National Museums Scotland, acc. no. A.1988.139 A to C

98. (FRONT)

(BACK)

101.

Now displayed as a panel, these embroideries were probably originally bed-hangings and show scenes of people dressed in French court fashions. Once believed to have been worked by the Four Maries while at Lochleven Castle, research has proved this to be impossible. The valance dates to the late 16th century, long after Mary's flight from Scotland.

102. MODEL OF MARY, QUEEN OF SCOTS

By Victoria Cairns, Scottish, 21st century
Lent by The Lady of Finavon

Few contemporary portraits of Mary exist, although many were done after her death. During her years in France, the court painter François Clouet provided a comprehensive record of Mary's early years, sketching her from the age of seven until her departure for Scotland. Clouet's drawings were the study for this particular model of Mary. The costume was inspired by a painting believed to be Mary, in the collection of Prince Czartoryski at Cracow, Poland.

103. MODEL OF HENRY STEWART, LORD DARNLEY

By Victoria Cairns, Scottish, 21st century
Lent by The Lady of Finavon

The artist has modelled Darnley's face from a painting by Hans Eworth. The costume is based on an engraving by Renold Elstraak, c.1566.

104. COSTUME SKETCHES FOR THE 1998 ENGLISH NATIONAL OPERA PRODUCTION OF DONIZETTI'S 'MARIA STUARDA'

By Jasper Conran, 1998
Mary's monochrome costume; Mary's monochrome costume with coat; Young Darnley's costume; Darnley's costume for the park scene; Mary's white costume; Elizabeth's leather costume; Mary's red costume
On loan courtesy of Jasper Conran OBE

Mary has been portrayed in books, verse, film, plays and opera. These exquisite sketches, created by the renowned fashion designer Jasper Conran, combine painstaking historical research with his own unique perspective.

105. SIGNET RING WITH ARMS OF MARY, QUEEN OF SCOTS, AS USED 1548–58

Possibly French, c.1548–58
Gold, chalcedony, enamels, c.2 cm (diameter)
Lent by The British Museum

This ring bears both the arms of Mary as Queen of Scots and an engraved cypher combining her initials with those of François, suggesting that it was made in France. It would have been used to seal official documents.

106. CAST OF THE SIGNET SEAL RING OF MARY, QUEEN OF SCOTS

Scottish, 19th century
Sulphur cast: glass seal 2 x 1.8 x 1.5 cm;
box 5.5 x 3.2 x 2.1 cm
National Museums Scotland, acc. no. H.NM 226

As part of the growing Romantic interest in Mary in the 19th century, glass casts of her signet ring [cat. no. 105] were also made for sale as 'relics' of the Queen.

107. *MINIATURE OF LORD JAMES STEWART, EARL OF MORAY (1531–70)*

Scottish, 19th century
Oil on copper, 6.2 x 4.6 x 4 cm
National Museums Scotland, acc. no. H.NT 271

Moray was an astute and skilled politician who acted as Mary's key adviser. Her marriage to Lord Darnley drove him to oppose her. On her abdication in 1567, he became Regent for the infant James VI.

107.

108. *ACTIS AND CONSTITUTIONIS*

Scottish, 1566
Book, 31.5 x 40 cm (open)
Lent by The British Library

This is a bound volume of all the Acts of the Scottish Parliament passed in 1566.

109. LICENCE SIGNED BY MARY, QUEEN OF SCOTS

Scottish, 1564
Paper, 30.5 x 26.5 cm
Lent by Dundee City Council

This licence, dated 11 September 1564, granted the burgh of Dundee permission to use monastery land for a new burial ground. The old cemetery within the town walls had become a health hazard. Mary attempted to promote the French practice of burying the dead outside the walled limits of towns and cities.

110.
(OBVERSE)

110.
(REVERSE)

112.

113.

110. CASTS OF OBVERSE AND REVERSE OF THE FIRST GREAT SEAL OF MARY, QUEEN OF SCOTS, *c.*1542

Scottish, 19th century
Red sulphur cast, 10.7 cm (diameter), 0.8 cm (depth)
National Museums Scotland, acc. no. K.1999.764
(obverse); K.1999.765 (reverse)

These casts show a stylised representation of the Queen on her throne and the Royal Arms of Scotland, *c.*1542. The Great Seal was used for authorising important documents such as royal land grants and appointments to high office.

111. CAST OF REVERSE OF SECOND GREAT SEAL OF MARY, QUEEN OF SCOTS, *c.*1544

Scottish, 19th century
Brown sulphur cast, 4.0 cm (diameter), 8 cm (depth)
National Museums Scotland, acc. no. K.1999.769

112. CAST OF REVERSE OF THE SECOND PRIVY SEAL OF MARY, QUEEN OF SCOTS, DEPICTING THE ROYAL ARMS, 1544

Scottish, 19th century
Brown sulphur cast, 7.1 cm (diameter), 0.8 cm (depth)
National Museums Scotland, acc. no. K.1999.787

The Privy Seal was used to authorise acts of the Privy Council.

113. CAST OF OBVERSE OF FOURTH GREAT SEAL OF MARY, QUEEN OF SCOTS, 1559

Scottish, 19th century
Red sulphur cast, 10.1 cm (diameter), 0.8 cm (depth)
National Museums Scotland, acc. no. K.1999.766

This depicts both Mary and her husband François, and the legend refers to them as King and Queen of France, Scotland, England and Ireland.

114. CAST OF THE OBVERSE AND REVERSE OF THE SEVENTH GREAT SEAL OF MARY, QUEEN OF SCOTS, 1564

Scottish, 19th century
Brown sulphur, 123 mm (diameter), 8 mm (depth)
National Museums Scotland, acc. no. K.1999.767 (obverse); K.1999.768 (reverse)

This depicts Mary as Queen of Scots and dowager Queen of France.

115. CHARTER, OF MARY, QUEEN OF SCOTS, IN FAVOUR OF HENRY BALNAVES, CONFIRMING HIM IN HIS LANDS IN FIFE, 13 MARCH 1566–67

Scottish, 16th century
Vellum with wax seal, 21.5 x 25 cm
Lent by National Records of Scotland

Henry Balnaves, a scholar and judge, professed the Protestant faith and originally received these lands from Cardinal Beaton in 1543 at a time when Beaton was trying to buy the support of opponents. Mary continued this policy of binding supporters to her by granting them lands. The date covers two years, as at this time the year changed in March, not January.

116. RYAL, OR NOBLE, OF MARY, QUEEN OF SCOTS

Minted in Edinburgh, 1555
Gold, 2.8 cm (diameter)
National Museums Scotland, acc. no. H.C4104

This coin was worth three pounds Scots.

117. SILVER JETON, OF MARY, QUEEN OF SCOTS

Minted in France, 1560
Silver, 3.2 cm (diameter)
National Museums Scotland, acc. no. H.R 4

A jeton was a token used to represent money. This one has Mary and François' arms on one side and the crowns of France and Scotland on the other.

116.
(OBVERSE)

(REVERSE)

117.
(OBVERSE)

(REVERSE)

118. *ACTIS AND CONSTITUTIONIS*

Edinburgh, 1563
Book, 28.5 x 40 cm (open)
The Faculty of Advocates
(see the National Library of Scotland)

The Act in this bound volume is known as the Witchcraft Act, which made both the practice of witchcraft and consulting with witches a capital offence. At the root of this legislation was a strong anti-Catholic impulse by the Reformers.

119. ARDSHEAL CHARMSTONE

Scottish, 16th to 17th century
Rock crystal ball with a silver frame and chain, 4.1 cm (diameter)
National Museums Scotland, acc. no. H.NO 72

Long associated with the Stewarts of Ardsheal, this charmstone was thought to ward off witches and to cure disease.

120. THE GLENORCHY CHARMSTONE

Scottish mount, early 17th century
Rock crystal with silver mount and pieces of coral, 7 x 4.5 cm
National Museums Scotland, acc. no. H.NO 118

This charmstone is said to have been worn by Sir Colin Campbell, Laird of Glenorchy, when fighting against the Turks in Rhodes. Mary believed in the power of charms and amulets. She sent her brother-in-law, Henri III of France, some charms along with her last letter.

121. THE BALLOCHYLE BROOCH

By William Stalker, Scottish, c.1610
Silver, rock crystal, 4.5 cm (height), 13.8 cm (diameter)
National Museums Scotland, acc. no. H.NGB 177

This brooch was in the possession of the MacIver-Campbell family of Ballochyle, Cowal, Argyll, who used it as a talisman against witchcraft and disease.

121.

A JOYOUS COURT

122. *MARY, QUEEN OF SCOTS*, IN OUTDOOR ATTIRE

Artist unknown, c.1560–92
Oil on panel, 25.1 x 19.1 cm
Lent by the National Portrait Gallery, London

This portrait of Mary has recently been rediscovered as an image painted within her lifetime or very shortly after her death. The painting was considered to date from the 18th century; however, recent tree-ring analysis has established that the wood which forms the panel was felled in the 16th century.

123. FRAGMENT OF SILK BRAID

Possibly French, date unknown
Silk, silver wire, 10 x 5 cm
National Museums Scotland, acc. no. A.1987.260

This was said to have been from a saddle which belonged to Mary, Queen of Scots.

124. PEREGRINE FALCON (*FALCO PEREGRINUS*) ON HAWKING GLOVE

Maker unknown, c.1850
Feathers, leather, 50 cm (height), 20 cm (width)
National Museums Scotland

Mary was a keen and accomplished hunter with hawks. She learned the art of hawking during her time in France. The peregrine falcon was the bird of choice for members of Europe's royal families, though Mary was said to favour the smaller merlin.

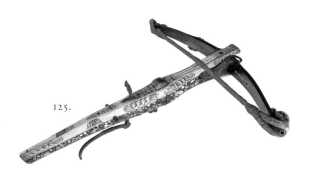

125.

125. CROSSBOW

German or Flemish, late 16th to early 17th century
Walnut stock, 59.7 cm (length); steel bow, 59.7 cm
(span), 3.8 cm (width), 1.3 cm (thick)
National Museums Scotland, acc. no. A.1905.615

The crossbow was the favoured bow for hunting as it was easier to handle than the longbow.

126. HARP OR CLARSACH

Maker unknown, Scottish, c.1450
Wood and brass, 81.2 x 51 cm
National Museums Scotland, acc. no. H.LT 1

This harp was traditionally said to have been given by Mary, Queen of Scots to Beatrix Gardyne of Banchory, while on a hunting trip to Atholl, c.1563. However, new research has revealed that this association is more likely to be because the harp's forepillar originally had a gold coin with a portrait of Mary fixed to it. Beatrix Gardyne married John Robertson of Monzie sometime before 1564 and the coin may have been added then to a treasured family heirloom, to emphasise the importance of this marriage.

126.

127. GOLD HALF RYAL OF MARY, QUEEN OF SCOTS

Minted in Edinburgh, 1555
Gold, 2.2 cm (diameter)
National Museums Scotland, acc. no. A.1911.506.1135

Worth 30 shillings Scots, the diameter of this portrait coin matches exactly the pattern of fixing nails left in the harp's pillar [see cat. no. 126].

127.

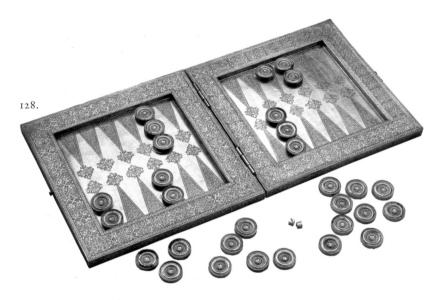

128.

128. GAMING BOARD WITH SILVER TABLE-MEN AND GOLD DICE

Maker unknown, possibly 16th century
Silver gilt, gold, 27.6 x 27.5 x 3.8 cm (closed)
On loan from a Private Collection

This gaming board is said to have been presented by Mary to Mary Seton, one of the Four Maries. The board is designed for playing backgammon, nine-men-morris, and chess or draughts.

129. VIRGINALS

Possibly Scottish, c.1560–1660
Wood (oak and spruce), 140 cm (height), 160 cm (length), 54 mm (width)
National Museums Scotland, acc. no. H.LT 122

Mary was fond of music and was able to play the virginals, a type of keyboard instrument on which, unlike the piano, the strings were plucked rather than struck. A set of virginals was commonly found in wealthy households. This instrument was said to have belonged to Lady Marie Stewart, Countess of Mar, daughter of James VI's favourite cousin, Esmé, Duke of Lennox.

130. TAPESTRY

Flemish, 16th century
Wool, 314 x 254 cm
National Museums Scotland, acc. no. A.1905.1019

During the 16th century, the most costly wall-hangings were those made of tapestry, a woven technique producing strong hangings which could take designs. Used to decorate rooms, they were often woven with allegorical, Biblical or historical scenes. The scene on this tapestry shows the Queen of Sheba before Solomon, an episode from one of the books of the Old Testament.

131. CABINET

French, mid-16th century
Oak, 210 x 179 x 80 cm
National Museums Scotland, acc. no. H.KL 104

This carved oak cabinet in Renaissance style, imported from France, is known as the Queen Mary cabinet from a belief that it belonged to Mary. It was for a long time in the keeping of the Hepburns of Smeaton, East Lothian, who supported her. There would not have been many pieces of furniture of this quality in 16th-century Scotland and it may indeed have come from one of the royal palaces.

129.

131.

132. NURSING CHAIR

Possibly Scottish, 16th to 17th century
Oak, 87.5 x 63.5 x 50 cm
Lent by The Earl of Mar and Kellie

This chair is traditionally said to have belonged to
Annabella Drummond, Countess of Mar, whose
initials 'AM' are carved on the back. The Earl and
Countess of Mar looked after James VI as a child.

THE QUEEN'S HUSBAND

133. *HENRY STEWART, LORD DARNLEY (1545–67)*

Attributed to Levina Teerlinc, Flemish, 1560
Watercolour on vellum, 6.2 x 5 cm (framed)
On loan courtesy of The Thomson Collection

This miniature of Darnley was painted while he
and his family were in exile in England under the
protection of Elizabeth I. Levina Teerlinc (*c*.1510–76)
was an accomplished court painter, and the commission demonstrates the high status of Darnley and his
family, the Lennox Stewarts.

134. THE DARNLEY RING

Possibly Scottish, 16th century with 19th-century
additions
Gold, 2.5 cm (diameter)
Lent by the Victoria and Albert Museum

This signet ring was said to have been found near
Fotheringhay Castle. It is engraved with the initials
'MH' and true lovers' knots, and was once thought
to have been Mary and Darnley's betrothal ring.
The inner engraving of the Royal Arms of Scotland
and Darnley's name were added in the 19th century.

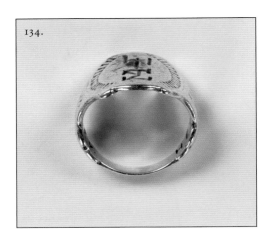

134.

135. REPLICA OF THE DARNLEY RING

Probably English, after 1857
Silver, 2.3 cm (diameter), 1.4 cm (height at bezel)
Lent by the Victoria and Albert Museum

These replicas of the original Darnley ring were
produced to cater to the many 19th-century
admirers of Mary, Scotland's romantic and tragic
heroine.

136. REPLICA OF THE DARNLEY RING

Probably English, after 1857
Silver, 1.9 cm (diameter), 1.5 cm (height)
National Museums Scotland, acc. no. K.2012.78

137. MEDAL TO CELEBRATE THE MARRIAGE OF MARY AND DARNLEY ON 29 JULY 1565

19th-century electrotype of mid-16th century original
Bronze, 4.3 cm (diameter), 3 cm (depth)
National Museums Scotland, acc. no. H.R 7

138. RYAL, OF HENRY AND MARY

Minted in Edinburgh, 1565
Silver, 4.3 cm (diameter)
National Museums Scotland, acc. no. K.2002.2116

This rare coin, known as the 'marriage ryal', bears an inscription which begins with Henry's name rather than Mary, who should have first place as Queen Regnant. Given his dynastic ambitions, there is some speculation that Darnley may have had a hand in this. These coins were quickly withdrawn from circulation.

139. RYAL, OF MARY AND HENRY

Minted in Edinburgh, 1566
Silver, 4.4 cm (diameter)
National Museums Scotland, acc. no. H.C403

The design on this coin of a tortoise climbing a crowned palm tree was well known to Mary; she embroidered it on the Marian Hanging (see page 56). Some speculate that it refers to Darnley's pretentions to the Crown Matrimonial.

140. RYAL, OF MARY AND HENRY

Minted in Edinburgh, 1567
Silver, 4.4 cm (diameter)
National Museums Scotland, acc. no. H.C408

This coin has the corrected version of the inscription on the 1565 ryal [cat. no. 138] as Mary's name comes before that of Darnley, her King Consort.

141. *HENRY STEWART, LORD DARNLEY (1545–67)*

Artist unknown, possibly English, c.1564
Oil on panel, 94.7 x 77.5 x 5 cm
Lent by the Scottish National Portrait Gallery, Edinburgh

Darnley is shown here in his late teens, shortly before his marriage to his cousin Mary, Queen of Scots in July 1565. Darnley was a direct descendant of both James II of Scotland and Henry VII of England. For Mary, this was a perfect dynastic match, as she had her own claim to the English throne. Though they were initially deeply in love, the marriage soon turned sour and ended with Darnley's unsolved murder in February 1567.

138.   139.   140.

142. TESTAMENTARY INVENTORY OF THE QUEEN'S JEWELS, BOOK, PLATE

May or June 1566
Ink on paper, 25 x 38.5 cm
Lent by National Records of Scotland

In the weeks before the birth of Prince James on 19 June 1566, Mary made her will. It was intended to take effect in the event of the death of both her and her unborn child during labour. Mary has written the names of the beneficiaries. Included on this page are two of the Four Maries – Seton and Beaton.

143. *MARTIN NUGGET, WINGATE NUGGET* AND FRESHWATER PEARLS

Martin Nugget (National Museums Scotland, acc. no. G.1994.20.4) – Straightsteps, Wanlockhead, Dumfriesshire; Wingate Nugget (G.13.10) – Wingate, Leadhills, Lanarkshire; freshwater pearls – River Tay, Perthshire (G.2005.129.2)

These two gold nuggets are from the area where gold was found that was used in the remodelling of the Scottish crown for James V. Scottish freshwater pearls were highly prized in Europe. Mary was particularly fond of pearls and had several pieces made with them.

PRINCE JAMES

144. PRINCE JAMES

Artist unknown
Oil on panel, 41.2 x 35 x 5 cm
Lent by the Scottish National Portrait Gallery, Edinburgh

Prince James was born, after a difficult birth, at Edinburgh Castle. Even the arrival of their son was not enough to save Mary and Darnley's failing marriage. Darnley did not attend his son's baptism at the Chapel Royal, Stirling Castle, on 17 December 1566.

144.

145. ORDER FROM CRAIGMILLAR CASTLE TO THE TREASURER TO SUPPLY TAFFETA FOR THE BAPTISM OF PRINCE JAMES

3 December 1566
Ink on paper, 31 x 21 cm
Lent by National Records of Scotland

The baptism of James was a hugely important event for Mary. It was the largest public celebration ever held in Scotland. Mary had to increase taxation to pay for the festivities which followed the baptismal service, conducted with the rites of the Catholic Church rather than the Reformed Kirk.

PRIME SUSPECT

146. GUITAR

Attributed to René Voboam, French, c.1650
Wood, ebony, ivory, 93.3 cm (length), 25.6 cm (width)
Lent by the Royal College of Music, London

146.

This guitar is typical of a number of objects which over the years have become associated with Mary and her court. It was in the possession of one family for many generations, with the romantic reputation that it had been given by Mary to David Rizzio.

147. MINUTE BOOK SHOWING TRIALS OF ROBERT CUNNINGHAM, ROBERT WATSON AND OTHERS FOR THEIR INVOLVEMENT IN DAVID RIZZIO'S MURDER

April 1566
Book, 22.5 x 32 x 3.5 cm; 33 x 48 cm (double page)
Lent by National Records of Scotland

The conspiracy to murder Rizzio was large, with 80 individuals involved. All were declared to be rebels and outlaws, and were forced to surrender their possessions to the Crown.

148. DOCUMENT PARDONING MORTON AND OTHERS OVER THE MURDER OF RIZZIO

24 December 1655
Ink on paper, 22.5 x 32 x 3.5 cm; 33 x 48 cm (double page)
Lent by National Records of Scotland

On Christmas Eve 1566, Mary pardoned the Earl of Morton and more than 70 of those implicated in the plot to murder Rizzio, many of whom had gone into exile to escape justice.

149. KEY

Scottish, 15th century
Iron, 18 cm (length), 5.8 cm (max. width), 1 cm (depth)
National Museums Scotland, acc. no. H.MJ 50

This door-key was found at Craigmillar Castle, Edinburgh. In November 1566 Craigmillar was the scene of discussions between Mary and her Lords as to how they might deal with the problem of the King. Mary refused to have Darnley's murder on her conscience. In her absence, her Lords signed the Craigmillar Bond, an agreement to murder Darnley.

MURDER AT KIRK O' FIELD

150. BIRD'S EYE VIEW OF KIRK O' FIELD

English, 1567
Ink on paper, 40 x 57.5 cm
Lent by The National Archives, UK

This sketch was drawn for William Cecil, Elizabeth's Secretary of State. It is an illustrated narrative of the events surrounding the murder and not merely a depiction of the murder scene. The bodies of Darnley and his servant are shown in larger scale, top right.

151. EARTHENWARE FRAGMENTS

French, 16th century
Clay, painted and glazed, 4 x 4.2 cm and 5.7 x 6.6 cm
Lent by Addyman Archaeology

In 2010 an archaeological dig was undertaken at the Old College of the University of Edinburgh. The Old College stands on the site of the Old Provost's Lodging, scene of the Darnley murder. These earthenware fragments come from a high-status object and were highly decorative. Other discoveries on the site included the remains of Hamilton House, a mansion built in 1552 for the Duke of Châtelherault.

152. GLASS FRAGMENT

Netherlandish, 16th century
Blown glass, 3.7 x 2.8 cm
Lent by Addyman Archaeology

This glass fragment formed the knop of a goblet, where the bowl joins the stem. The lion-head decoration is still visible on this expensive example of glassware.

AFTERMATH

153. *JAMES HEPBURN, 4TH EARL OF BOTHWELL (c.1535–78)*

Artist unknown, Scottish, 1566
Oil on copper, 3.7 cm (diameter)
Lent by the Scottish National Portrait Gallery, Edinburgh
Gifted by the Society of Antiquaries in 2009

This is one of a pair of miniatures commemorating the wedding of Bothwell and Lady Jean Gordon in 1566. Mary's increasing reliance on Bothwell, his implication in the murder of Darnley, and their marriage in May 1567 after he divorced Jean Gordon, led to Mary's downfall.

154. *MERMAID AND HARE*

Artist unknown, 1567
Ink on paper, 30.2 x 21.5 cm
Lent by The National Archives, UK

These anonymous satirical placards circulated around Edinburgh shortly after the murder of Darnley in March 1567, and refer to the alleged adulterous relationship between Mary 'M[aria] R[egina]' and the Earl of Bothwell. Mary was represented as a mermaid, a symbol of prostitution in 16th-century Europe. Bothwell was represented by a hare, part of his family crest. This placard was sent by an English spy to Elizabeth I's ministers in England.

IN PURSUIT OF A QUEEN

155. BANNER DESIGN USED AT CARBERRY HILL

Scottish, 1567
Ink on paper, 32 x 45.5 cm
Lent by The National Archives, UK

This is a sketch made of a banner used by the Lords of the Congregation at Carberry Hill near Edinburgh during their confrontation with Mary and her forces on 15 June 1567. It depicts the body of Darnley, and the infant Prince James praying for God to avenge his father's murder.

156. WATERCOLOUR OF ENCOUNTER AT CARBERRY

Scottish, 1567
Watercolour, 40.5 x 57 cm
Lent by The National Archives, UK

This image represents the stand-off between the forces of Mary, Queen of Scots and her third husband, the Earl of Bothwell, against the Lords of the Congregation at Carberry Hill. Mary surrendered and was imprisoned in Lochleven Castle.

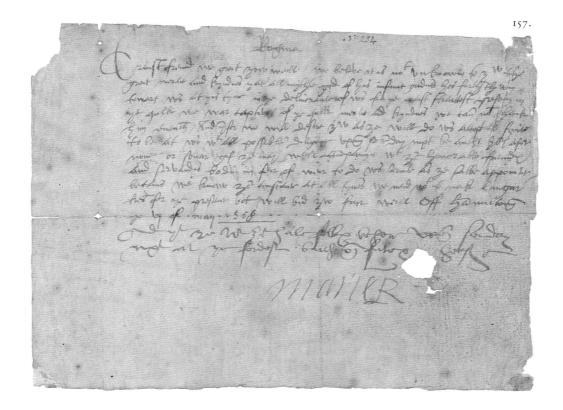

157. LETTER SENT TO THE LAIRD OF ADAMTOUN REQUIRING HIS ATTENDANCE AT HAMILTON, WITH THE AUTOGRAPH SIGNATURE OF MARY, QUEEN OF SCOTS

6 May 1568
Paper, 15.5 x 21 cm
National Museums Scotland, acc. no. H.OA 8

This letter was sent only four days after Mary's escape from Lochleven Castle, as she rallied her supporters to her temporary court at Hamilton, in anticipation of the impending battle with the Lords.

THE LENNOX STEWARTS AND THE DARNLEY MEMORIAL

158. THE MEMORIAL OF LORD DARNLEY

By Livinus de Vogelaare, Flemish, 1567
Oil on canvas, 142.3 x 224 cm
Lent by the Royal Collection Trust on behalf of Her Majesty the Queen

This painting, commissioned by the parents of Darnley, the Earl and Countess of Lennox, highlights the murder of an apparently pious son and makes it very clear who they held responsible for his death. The grieving parents kneel at the tomb of their son, with their grandson, Prince James, the future King James, in front of them. Behind them is their younger son, Charles.

The tomb has two reliefs: one showing the murder of Darnley and his servant as they are dragged from their beds; the other depicting their dead bodies. Mary's surrender to the Lords of the Congregation at Carberry Hill on 15 June 1567 can be seen in the bottom left-hand corner. As a propaganda painting, it is a damning condemnation of Mary's alleged role in the murder of her husband, and her inappropriate relationship with the Earl of Bothwell.

159. THE DARNLEY OR LENNOX JEWEL

Maker unknown, possibly Scottish, c.1571–78
Gold, enamel, Burmese rubies, Indian emerald and
cobalt-blue glass, 7.6 cm (height with pendant loop),
5.2 cm (width)
Lent by the Royal Collection Trust on behalf of Her
Majesty the Queen

Little is known about the origin of this heart-shaped
locket, other than its association with the Lennox
family. It may have been commissioned as a memorial piece by the Countess of Lennox, to her husband,
the Earl of Lennox, who was killed in 1571. It could
have been made either to commemorate the Earl's
return to Scotland, or to mark the restoration of his
lands and honours in 1564–65. Although it is uncer-
tain where it was made, the high quality of the work-
manship was of the calibre found in Edinburgh in
the 1570s. Three Edinburgh goldsmiths were certainly capable of such work: George Heriot, Michael
Gilbert II or James Gray. It is one of the most
important early jewels in the Royal Collection.

THE ROAD TO ABDICATION

160. LOCHLEVEN HANGING

Scottish, early 17th century
Wool, velvet appliqué, silk embroidery, 175 x 94 cm
National Museums Scotland, acc. no. A.1921.68

Many artefacts have become associated with Mary.
It was thought that this hanging was worked by her
during her imprisonment at Lochleven Castle from
June 1567 to May 1568. However, research has
proved that the hanging is of a later date.

161. KEY-RING AND KEYS

Scottish, 16th century
Iron: belt hook, 13.2 cm (length), 5.7 cm (max. width),
2.2 cm (max. depth); largest key 11.2 cm (length), 4 cm
(max. width), 2.2 cm (max. depth); smallest key 8.3 cm
(length), 3.4 cm (max. width), 0.6 cm (max. depth)
National Museums Scotland, acc. no. H.MJ 57

This key-ring and set of 8 keys were found near
Lochleven Castle, where Mary escaped from on 2
May 1568. It was reported that the keys used to free
her were thrown away.

162. *JAMES HEPBURN, 4TH EARL OF BOTH-WELL (c.1535–78) (STUDY OF MUMMIFIED HEAD)*

By Otto Bache, Danish, 19th century
Oil on canvas, 28.7 x 27.3 cm (unframed)
Lent by the Scottish National Portrait Gallery, Edinburgh

After Carberry Hill, Bothwell fled to Denmark,
where he was arrested and imprisoned in Malmö
Castle for breach of a marriage contract with Anna
Throndsen, a Danish noblewoman. He was kept
in appalling conditions and died ten years later.
Bothwell's remains are now buried in the church
there.

MARY'S FLIGHT FROM SCOTLAND

163. LETTER TO THE LAIRD OF SMEATON, SIGNED BY MARY, QUEEN OF SCOTS

Sent from Carlisle, 25 June 1568
Paper, 19.6 x 28.6 cm (unmounted)
National Museums Scotland, acc. no. H.OA 161

Mary arrived in England on 16 May 1568. Two days
later she was escorted to Carlisle Castle, where she
was held for the next two months.

160.

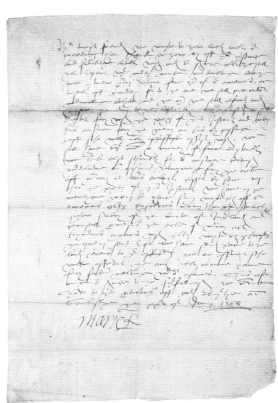

163.

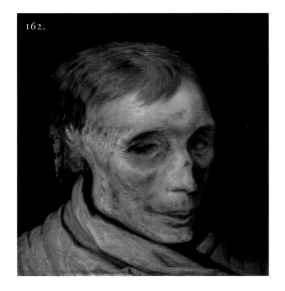

162.

161.

164. INVENTORY OF THE QUEEN'S CLOTHING SENT TO LOCHLEVEN CASTLE

5 May 1568, ink on paper, 30.8 x 21 cm (unmounted)
Lent by National Records of Scotland

These items were received after Mary had escaped from Lochleven. Mary's servant notes in a receipt that they were put in a chest so that they could be taken to the Queen if required.

THE CASKET LETTERS

165. MINUTE BOOK

Edinburgh, 16 September 1568
Bound volume, 44.5 x 58.5 cm
Lent by National Records of Scotland

This minute book records the moment James Douglas, Earl of Morton, produced a casket at the Scottish Privy Council. It supposedly contained letters written by Mary to Bothwell. The casket is described in the minutes as 'Ane Silver box owergilt with gold'.

166. CASKET LETTER

Facsimile of the original, paper, 27.5 x 31.1 x 22.2 cm
Lent by The National Archives, UK

This is the first page of a copy of an English translation of the longest of the casket letters. It was presented in 1568 to the commission investigating Mary's involvement in Darnley's murder. The original was alleged to have been written between 1566 and 1567. This facsimile is a poor copy, roughly translated from French, and only includes excerpts from one of the originals. This adds to the many doubts over the authenticity of these letters.

167. CASKET

Maker unknown, French, 15th century
Silver gilt, 25.4 x 15.2 x 10.1 cm
Lent by His Grace The Duke of Hamilton, Lennoxlove, Haddington

This casket has been in the Hamilton Collection since the 1670s. It is said to have contained the famous Casket Letters that allegedly implicated Mary in the murder of Darnley.

QUEENS AND COUSINS

168. MODEL OF ELIZABETH I, c.1592

By Victoria Cairns, Scottish, 21st century
Lent by The Lady of Finavon

This model is inspired by the Harwick portrait of Elizabeth by Nicholas Hilliard. By studying the painting, the artist drew the animals, fish, birds and flowers to scale. These were then drawn onto silk fabric and painstakingly embroidered onto the skirt. There are various opinions on whether the skirt was embroidered or painted. After consulting the work of the renowned costume historian, Janet Arnold, the artist agreed that the skirt was embroidered.

169. MODEL OF MARY, QUEEN OF SCOTS, c.1566

By Victoria Cairns, Scottish, 21st century
Lent by The Lady of Finavon

170. PLAN OF TUTBURY CASTLE

By John Somers, English, 31 December 1584
Paper, 32 x 21.5 cm
Lent by The British Library

This plan of Tutbury Castle was drawn up by one of Mary's gaolers just before she returned there in January 1585. Tutbury was her least favourite prison. The castle was in a poor state of repair; it was cold, damp and affected by noxious smells from nearby marshy ground. These conditions were extremely detrimental to Mary's health.

171.

171. CRUCIFIX

French, 16th century
Gold and enamel, *c.*6.4 cm (height)
By kind permission of His Grace The Duke of Norfolk

This crucifix was given by Mary, Queen of Scots to John Feckenham, the last Abbot of Westminster Abbey, London. It also contains a relic of the 'True Cross'.

172. THE HERRIES BOOK OF HOURS

French, late 16th century
Ink on parchment, 23 x 12 cm
By kind permission of The Lady Herries of Terregles

This illuminated Book of Hours was reputed to have been left by Mary at Terregles, Dumfriesshire, during her flight to England and captivity. Terregles was the home of Lord Herries, a prominent supporter.

173. BOOK OF HOURS

Printed by Robert Granjon, Lyon, 1558
Book, 16 x 9 x 1.7 cm (closed)
Lent by the British Province of the Society of Jesus

This Book of Hours was printed for Queen Mary I of England. It is said to have been in the possession of Mary, Queen of Scots at her execution at Fotheringhay Castle on 8 February 1587. It is thought that the book was given to Elizabeth Curle, one of Mary's female attendants, just before the execution.

174. THE HOLY THORN RELIQUARY OF MARY, QUEEN OF SCOTS

Maker unknown, early 17th century
Gold, 30 x 10 x 10 cm
Lent by the British Province of the Society of Jesus

This reliquary contains a holy thorn, said to have been taken from the crown of thorns placed upon Christ's head at his Crucifixion. A gift from her father-in-law, King Henri II, Mary brought this relic back to Scotland. Tradition claims that this holy thorn was given by Mary to Thomas Percy, 7th Earl of Northumberland, a prominent English Catholic.

175.

175. RING

Maker unknown, possibly 16th century
Gold, sapphire
Lent by His Grace The Duke of Hamilton, Lennoxlove, Haddington

This ring bears an inscription on the back of the bezel and the hoop: 'Sent by Queen Mary of Scotland at her death to John, Mar(quis) Hamilton.' It was probably added in the 17th century. John, 1st Marquis of Hamilton, was a staunch supporter of Mary. He went into exile after Mary's defeat at the Battle of Langside in May 1568.

176. POMANDER

Maker unknown, c.1600
Silver gilt, 4.1 x 2.5 cm
Lent by the Royal Collection Trust on behalf of Her
Majesty the Queen

This pomander is said to have belonged to Mary, Queen of Scots. A pomander would have contained a perfumed substance to keep bad smells at bay. However, they were often filled with incense to aid the wearer in their prayers and devotions.

177. SCISSORS AND CASE

Unknown provenance, possibly 16th century
Silver, 6.8 cm (length), 3.4 cm (width), 0.6 cm (depth)
National Museums Scotland, acc. no. H.RHM 1

This small pair of scissors, contained in a delicate ornamental filigree case, has long been associated with Mary, who was an accomplished needle-worker.

178. THE MARIAN HANGING

English, 1570–85
Silk velvet, panels of canvas work, embroidered in silks
and silver-gilt thread, 227 x 292 cm
Lent by the Victoria and Albert Museum

This wall-hanging is thought to have been made by Mary and the Countess of Shrewsbury, better known as Bess of Hardwick, wife of the Earl of Shrewsbury, Mary's principal gaoler. The hanging consists of embroidered panels on a green velvet background, which depict a variety of plants and animals. The central panel has a Latin inscription that translates as 'Virtue Flourishes by Wounding'. The octagonal panel above this bears the crown and thistle emblem of Scotland, with Mary's monogram, the letters 'MA', superimposed on the Greek letter *phi*. The embroideries were sewn together after her death.

KING'S AND QUEEN'S MEN

179. *JAMES STEWART, 1ST EARL OF MORAY*

By Hans Eworth, Flemish, 1561
Oil on panel, 86.6 x 70.5 x 7 cm
On loan from a Private Collection

This portrait of the Earl of Moray was possibly commissioned for the occasion of his marriage to Lady Agnes Keith in 1561. Moray was Regent of Scotland from August 1567 until his assassination in January 1570.

180. THE ERSKINE EWER

By James Cok II, Scottish, 1565–68
Cut and polished rock crystal, silver-gilt mounts,
24 cm (height), 10 cm (diameter of base)
The Bute Collection at Mount Stuart

The arms of John Erskine, Earl of Mar, a supporter of Mary and therefore a Queen's man, are engraved on the lid of this ewer. Mar later turned against Mary. James Cok, who made the ewer, and James Mosman, two Edinburgh goldsmiths and supporters of Mary, pawned jewels to raise cash to prolong Scotland's civil war. They were executed in 1573 for their part in the 'lang siege' of Edinburgh Castle.

181. JACK OR BRIGANDINE

Probably English, late 16th century
Steel, linen, 58.5 x 50.8 cm (laced up)
National Museums Scotland, acc. no. A.1905.485

This protective doublet was the typical armour for rank and file soldiers from the medieval period up until the later 16th century. It consists of small overlapping steel plates tied to a body of canvas padded with linen layers.

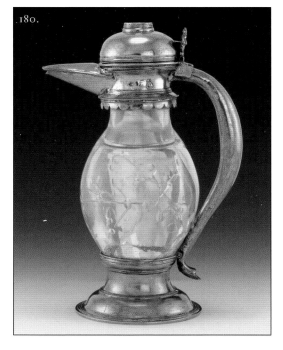

180.

181.

182.

182. HELMET

Italian, late 16th century
Iron, 17.5 cm (height), 26.5 x 22 cm (brim)
National Museums Scotland, acc. no. H.LN 50

This style of helmet, known as a Spanish morion, was commonly used in Scotland during the 16th century. This example was found at Manton Walls at Ancrum in Roxburghshire.

183. *GEORGE BUCHANAN (1506–82)*

Artist unknown, late 16th century
Oil on panel, 25.4 (diam.); 31.2 x 31.5 x 3.4 cm (framed)
Lent by the Scottish National Portrait Gallery, Edinburgh

Once a staunch supporter of Mary, Buchanan turned against her in the aftermath of Darnley's murder. When he became tutor to the young James VI, he tried to indoctrinate him with highly critical views of James's mother, Mary. Buchanan was also notorious for the beatings he administered to his pupil.

184. *ANE DETECTION OF THE DUINGS OF MARIE QUENE OF SCOTTES TOUCHAND THE MURDER OF HER HUSBAND*

By George Buchanan, Edinburgh, 1571
Book, 14.5 x 18.7 cm (open)
Lent by the National Library of Scotland

Originally published in Latin, this edition, in imitation Scots, was intended to promote Buchanan's opinions of Mary's guilt to a wider audience. Buchanan, who had previously written Mary's masques performed at Holyroodhouse and Stirling, bitterly claimed that she was 'a woman raging without measure or modesty'.

185. *DE ORIGINE MORIBUS, ET REBUS GESTIS SCOTORUM*

By Bishop John Leslie, Rome, 1578
Line engraving on paper, 20.6 x 14.6 cm
Lent by the Scottish National Portrait Gallery, Edinburgh

Leslie, Bishop of Ross, was a loyal, yet not uncritical, supporter of Mary. In this book illustration, Leslie still referred to James as 'Prince', 11 years after Mary's forced abdication. To Leslie she was still Queen.

THE BABINGTON PLOT

186. THE CORONATION PORTRAIT OF QUEEN ELIZABETH I OF ENGLAND

Artist unknown, English, c.1600
Oil on panel, 127.3 x 99.7 cm
Lent by the National Portrait Gallery, London

Elizabeth was painted in the cloth of gold that she wore at her coronation on 15 January 1559. Previously it had been worn by her half-sister, Mary I. She holds the orb and sceptre, symbols of her royal authority, and the English crown is firmly placed on her head.

187. *WILLIAM CECIL, 1ST BARON BURGHLEY*

Artist unknown, c.1585
Oil on panel, 54.6 x 44.5 cm
Lent by the National Portrait Gallery, London

Cecil (1520–98), Elizabeth's principal Secretary of State, was dedicated to his Queen's service and safety. This devotion influenced his treatment of Mary. He had wanted to put her on trial when she first arrived in England in 1568.

188. QUEEN ELIZABETH, SIR WILLIAM CECIL AND SIR FRANCIS WALSINGHAM

Artist unknown, possibly early 17th century
Line engraving, 19 x 15 cm
Lent by the National Portrait Gallery, London

This later representation shows Elizabeth flanked by her two most trusted and loyal advisers, who guided her policies during the time of Mary's imprisonment in England.

189. SIR FRANCIS WALSINGHAM (c.1532–90)

Possibly after John de Critz the Elder, c.1587
Oil on panel, 37.5 x 29.8 cm
Lent by the National Portrait Gallery, London

Walsingham established and led the Elizabethan secret service, which provided a stream of intelligence for William Cecil. His efforts, mainly directed against Roman Catholic conspirators, were fuelled by his zealous Protestant faith. He believed the main threat to his Queen and her realm was 'the devilish woman' – his view of Mary. Through the opportunity of the Babington Plot, Walsingham was able to seal Mary's ultimate fate.

190. CODED CIPHERS

English, 1586
Ink on paper, 31.3 x 23.6 cm
Lent by The National Archives, UK

This document is Mary's alphabet of ciphers. It was discovered at Chartley, a manor house in Staffordshire where Mary was imprisoned during the course of the Babington Plot. At this time, Mary could only communicate with the outside world secretly. Her communications were encrypted by her cipher secretary, Gilbert Curle. The encoded messages were then smuggled out of Chartley to her supporters.

191. BABINGTON POSTSCRIPT AND CIPHER

English, 1586
Ink on paper, 30.3 x 20.2 cm
Lent by The National Archives, UK

This is the postscript and cipher Walsingham used as evidence against the Babington plotters and Mary. Thomas Phelippes, Walsingham's leading code-breaker, had deciphered the simple formula used by Mary. He copied one of Mary's intercepted letters to the Catholic conspirator, Anthony Babington. He then added this postscript to the letter, asking Babington to tell Mary the names of the other conspirators. Mary had played into Walsingham's hands.

192. THE TRIAL OF MARY, QUEEN OF SCOTS

Artist unknown, 15 October 1586
Ink and pencil, 51 x 39.5 cm
Lent by The British Library

This narrative sketch of the trial is from the papers of Robert Beale, Clerk to the Privy Council. Mary is shown twice: first, entering the hall with two of her ladies, and second, seated on the right of the empty chair of state, which represented the absent Elizabeth I.

193. COPY OF THE DEATH WARRANT OF MARY, QUEEN OF SCOTS

1 February 1587
Paper, 35 x 23.5 cm
Lent by His Grace The Archbishop of Canterbury and the Trustees of Lambeth Palace Library

The original warrant disappeared in the recriminations that followed Mary's execution. This copy was delivered to Robert Beale by Henry Grey, 6th Earl of Kent, one of the two commissioners tasked with organising the execution.

194. PRIVY COUNCIL LETTER TO HENRY
GREY, 6TH EARL OF KENT, ORDERING THE
ENACTMENT OF THE WARRANT FOR THE
EXECUTION OF MARY, QUEEN OF SCOTS

3 February 1587
Paper, 31.2 x 20.2 cm
Lent by His Grace The Archbishop of Canterbury and
the Trustees of Lambeth Palace Library

The death warrant was accompanied by this covering
letter to the Earl from the Privy Council.

195. LETTER BY JAMES VI TO ELIZABETH I,
SEEKING MERCY FOR HIS MOTHER, MARY

26 January 1587
Paper, 32.5 x 23.5 cm
Lent by The British Library

James had to tread a very careful path once the
decision had been made to execute his mother. If
he was overly protective of her, he might forfeit his
right to succeed Elizabeth. However, if he remained
inactive, this would not play well in Scotland. In
the end his dynastic ambitions held sway; he made
his protest and suggested that Elizabeth exile Mary.

196. *THE EXECUTION OF MARY, QUEEN OF
SCOTS*

Artist unknown, 8 February 1587
Ink and pencil, 51 x 39.5 cm
Lent by The British Library

Also from the papers of Robert Beale, this sketch
shows Mary three times: entering the great hall; being
attended by her chamber-women on the scaffold; and,
finally, lying at the block with the executioner's axe
raised, ready to strike.

197. *THE EXECUTION OF MARY, QUEEN OF
SCOTS*

Artist unknown, Netherlandish, early 17th century
Watercolour on paper, 21.9 x 26.4 cm
Lent by the Scottish National Portrait Gallery,
Edinburgh

Although this watercolour was painted some years
after the execution, it does reflect the written
accounts of eye-witnesses and the drawings prepared
for Robert Beale. The burning of Mary's clothes,
shown in the far left of the scene, was intended to
prevent her supporters from keeping them as relics
of her martyrdom.

198. *A TRUE NARRATION OF THE EXECUTION
OF MARY, LATE QUEEN OF SCOTLAND,
WITHIN THE CASTLE OF FOTHERINGHAY.*

By Sir Robert Wingfield, 8 February 1587
Book, 19 x 13 cm (closed)
The Bute Collection at Mount Stuart

This eye-witness account of the execution was compiled by Sir Robert Wingfield, a nephew of William
Cecil. Sir Robert, a wealthy Northamptonshire
gentleman, was also involved with the arrangements
for Mary's funeral at Peterborough Cathedral in
August 1587.

199. DRAFT LETTER FROM JAMES VI TO
ELIZABETH I ABOUT HIS MOTHER'S
EXECUTION

March 1587
Paper, 29.5 x 21 cm
Lent by The British Library

Contemporary accounts reveal that James reacted
in a variety of ways to the news of his mother's
execution – from outbursts of anger to reflective
sadness. In this draft letter, written only a month
after his mother's death, James's concern is to
maintain a good relationship with Elizabeth.

200. *MARY, QUEEN OF SCOTS*

By Thomas de Leu, French, late 16th century
Line engraving, 23.4 x 18.1 x 3.9 cm (framed)
Lent by Sir Angus Grossart

It is not certain if this print was produced during Mary's lifetime. However, it is a clear indication of the interest that surrounded her in France, even after she returned to Scotland.

201. *MARTYRE DE LA ROYNE D'ECOSSE*

By Adam Blackwood, Edinburgh, 1587
Paper, 17.5 x 22.4 x 4 cm (open)
National Museums Scotland (Library), LIB 241

One of the better-known examples of the many printed memorials that appeared after Mary's death, Blackwood's version of the execution was based in part on the testimonies of Mary's chamber-women who were present with her on the scaffold.

202. *LA MORTE DE LA ROYNE D'ECOSSE*

By Adam Blackwood, Edinburgh, 1589
Book, 11 x 17 x 2 cm (open)
National Museums Scotland (Library), LIB 246

Blackwood expanded the account of Mary's treatment at the hands of Elizabeth in this memorial volume. He bemoaned the execution of his Queen by barbarous and tyrannical cruelty in this contribution to the debate that raged around Mary's memory.

203. *MARY, QUEEN OF SCOTS*

By Pieter Stevens van Gunst, after Adriaen van der Werff, 1697
Line engraving, 40.2 x 26.2 x 2.3 cm (framed)
Lent by Sir Angus Grossart

This 17th-century engraving is evidence that even over a century after her execution there was still an abiding interest in Mary as a martyred queen.

204.

(DETAIL)

204. CASKET

Made by D. Simpson or Daniel Sutherland, Scottish, early 19th century
Silver, 4.5 x 2.3 x 2.5 cm
National Museums Scotland, acc. no. H.MEQ 601

This casket is engraved: 'Sacred to the memory of Mary Stuart, Queen of Scots.' As is typical with mementoes of this type, it contains a lock of hair said to be Mary's. During the 19th century, Mary, Queen of Scots was increasingly portrayed as Scotland's ultimate romantic heroine.

205. LOCKET

Maker unknown, probably Scottish, 18th or early 19th century
Silver, 3.2 x 1.5 x 0.4 cm
With acknowledgment to the owners, who are descendants of Sir John Young of Leny

Family tradition states that Mary gave this lock of hair to an ancestor, Sir John Young of Leny, who accompanied her from France in 1561.

206. SEAL MATRIX PENDANT

Maker unknown, probably Scottish
Gold, cairngorm, 3.5 x 2.1 x 2.6 cm
National Museums Scotland, acc. no. H.NM 239

This commemorative object has a tiny portrait of Mary, Queen of Scots.

207. CAMEOS

Maker unknown, 16th century
Onyx, 2.8 cm (height) and 1.9 cm (height)
Lent by The British Museum

These two portrait cameos were made to commemorate Mary in the years immediately after her execution in 1587.

208. CAMEO PENDANTS

Maker unknown, probably French, late 16th century
Paris, Bibliothèque nationale de France, département des Monnaies, médailles et antiques

209. BOX

Maker unknown, probably English, 1820–30
Gold, copper horn and glass, 8.5 x 6.7 x 2.6 cm
National Museums Scotland, acc. no. H.NQ 308

An inscription records that this box was given by Sir Charles Forbes, Baronet, to his friend, Colin Robertson, on 1st August 1834, and was from the collection of King George IV.

210. *KING JAMES VI AND I (1566–1625)*

By John de Critz, Flemish/English, 1604
Oil on canvas, 140 x 95 x 11 cm
Lent by the Scottish National Portrait Gallery, Edinburgh
Bequeathed by Sir James Naesmyth in 1897

This portrait of James was completed by one of the court's leading painters not long after James's accession to the English throne in 1603. The painting was commissioned to commemorate the Union of the Crowns and is notable for the fact that the King is depicted wearing the jewel known as 'The Mirror of Great Britain' on his hat.

211. REPLICA TOMB

After Cornelius and William Cure, English, the original between 1606 and 1612
Plaster, 150 x 230 x 120 cm
Lent by the Scottish National Portrait Gallery, Edinburgh

This is a replica of the original elaborate tomb erected at Westminster Abbey in London, by James VI and I. Mary's body was moved to Westminster Abbey in October 1612 from its original place of interment at Peterborough Cathedral. Her final resting-place was to be in Henry VII's Chapel, along with her cousin, Elizabeth I. Tellingly, Mary's is the larger and more expensive of the two tombs. Perhaps this whole exercise was James's attempt to assuage his guilt at distancing himself from his mother during her lifetime.

211.

IMAGE CREDITS

For credit information about images used in chapters I–III, see pages X–XI. Images used within the Exhibition Catalogue section of this book are credited below.

© National Museums Scotland

catalogue nos 2, 13, 14, 24, 32, 34, 35, 36, 45, 48, 49, 52, 53, 56, 58, 60, 61, 67, 70, 71, 74, 77, 80, 81, 82, 86, 87, 92, 93, 95, 99, 102, 108, 111, 113, 114, 117, 118, 122, 126, 127, 128, 130, 132, 139, 140, 141, 158, 161, 162, 164, 182, 183, 206, 213

© National Galleries of Scotland

catalogue no. 213

Scottish National Portrait Gallery

catalogue nos 16, 163

© National Library of Scotland

for catalogue no. 18 (Adv MS.31.4.2 f.19)

© National Records of Scotland

for catalogue no. 10 (SP 13/80)

© Blairs Museum Trust

for catalogue no. 7

The Bute Collection at Mount Stuart

for catalogue no. 181

By kind permission of The Lady Herries of Terregles

for catalogue no. 173

© In the Collection of Lennoxlove, Haddington

for catalogue no. 176

© National Trust Images / John Hammond

for catalogue no. 179

© From Private Collections

for catalogue nos 72, 129

© RMN–Grand Palais (musée du Louvre) / Daniel Arnaudet, for catalogue no. 5

Royal College of Music

for catalogue no. 147

© Victoria and Albert Museum, London

for catalogue nos 6, 135, 179

FURTHER READING

Bath, Michael, *Emblems for a Queen: The Needle-work of Mary Queen of Scots* (London 2008).

Bingham, Caroline, *Darnley: A Life of Henry Stuart, Lord Darnley, Consort of Mary, Queen of Scots* (London 1995).

Donaldson, Gordon, *The First Trial of Mary, Queen of Scots* (London 1969).

Doran, Susan, *Mary, Queen of Scots: An Illustrated Life* (The British Library 2007).

Fraser, Antonia, *Mary, Queen of Scots* (London 1969).

Guy, John, *My Heart is my Own: The Life of Mary, Queen of Scots* (London 2004).

Marshall, Rosalind K., *John Knox* (Edinburgh 2000).

Marshall, Rosalind K., *Mary of Guise* (Edinburgh 2001).

Marshall, Rosalind K., Queen Mary's Women: *Female Relatives, Servants, Friends and Enemies of Mary, Queen of Scots* (Edinburgh 2006)

Merriman, Marcus, *The Rough Wooings: Mary, Queen of Scots* (East Linton 2000).

Smailes, Helen and Duncan Thomson, *The Queen's image: a celebration of Mary, Queen of Scots* (Edinburgh 1987).

Stewart, Alan, *The Cradle King: A Life of James VI and I* (London 2003).

Watkins, Susan, *Mary Queen of Scots* (London 2009).

Wormald, Jenny, *Mary, Queen of Scots: Politics, Passion and a Kingdom Lost* (London 2001).